**NEW EDITION**

# LADO ENGLISH SERIES

## WORKBOOK

### Robert Lado

Professor of Linguistics Emeritus and Former Dean
School of Languages and Linguistics
Georgetown University

Former Director
English Language Institute
University of Michigan

*in collaboration with*

JANN HUIZENGA     BERNADETTE SHERIDAN, I.H.M.
JEROME C. FORD     ANNETTE SILVERIO-BORGES

**PRENTICE HALL REGENTS**, Englewood Cliffs, New Jersey 07632

Editorial production supervision: Louisa B. Hellegers
Editorial development supervision: Deborah Goldblatt
Editorial development: Deborah Brennan
Interior design/page layout: A Good Thing Inc.
Design supervision: Janet Schmid
Pre-press buyer: Ray Keating
Manufacturing buyer: Lori Bulwin

Cover design: Janet Schmid
Cover photograph: © Slide Graphics of New England, Inc.

Illustrations by Constance Maltese

 © 1990, 1977, 1970 by Prentice Hall Regents
Prentice-Hall, Inc.
A Paramount Communications Company
Englewood Cliffs, New Jersey 07632

Printed in the United States of America

10  9  8  7

ISBN  0-13-522509-4

Prentice Hall International (UK) Limited, *London*
Prentice Hall of Australia Pty. Limited, *Sydney*
Prentice Hall Canada, Inc., *Toronto*
Prentice Hall Hispanoamericana, S.A., *Mexico*
Prentice Hall of India Private Limited, *New Delhi*
Prentice Hall of Japan, Inc., *Tokyo*
Simon & Schuster Asia Pte. Ltd., *Singapore*
Editora Prentice Hall do Brasil, Ltda., *Rio de Janeiro*

# CONTENTS

# PREFACE

The new edition of the *Lado English Series* is a complete six-level course in English. Each level is carefully graded and consists of a Student Book, Workbook, Teacher's Edition, and Audio Program. The main objective of the series is to help students understand, speak, read, and write English and to use these four skills for meaningful communication and interaction.

The new *Lado English Series* takes a balanced approach to teaching and learning. It offers a wide variety of techniques and activities -- including conversations and discussions, study frames and contextualized grammar exercises, listening and interaction activities, reading and role plays -- to help students learn English. The more controlled, structured exercises focus attention on learning the grammatical rules of English, while the freer, more open-ended activities offer ways of improving language skills through creative, spontaneous interaction.

This new edition retains the careful grading, simple presentation, and transparent organization that are classic trademarks of the *Lado English Series*. At the same time, several new features make this edition more modern and easier to use. The revised Student Book format features a larger type size, bigger pages, updated and extended content, and new art. For greater convenience, the Listening, Read, and Pronunciation sections have been moved from the Workbooks to the Students Books. Cassette symbols appear throughout the Student Books to identify the recorded material.

The exercises in the six Workbooks correspond to and complement the material covered in the Student Books. They offer additional exercises to help students master the material in each unit and focus on vocabulary, reading, and writing. In this new edition, controlled composition appears in all six Workbooks. In addition, review units with pre- and post-inventory tests are now included at the end of each Workbook. Answers to all Workbook activities can be found in an answer key at the back of the Teacher's Edition.

## Notes to the Teacher

Workbook 6 has ten units that correspond to the ten units in Student Book 6. The units are divided into the following six sections: Complete, Write, Read, Word Game, Vocabulary in Context, and Composition. The units are designed to strengthen the development of the different language skills. All activities can be done either as classwork or homework.

Each unit begins with a **Complete** section, which the students should do after they have mastered the conversation that opens the Student Book unit.

- Have the students look at the pictures to recall the situation. Teachers who are doing the activity in class may wish to ask individual students to identify the characters. Another option is to read aloud the description of the situation given in the Teacher's Edition.
- Ask the students to read the conversation silently and then complete it, either in class or at home. Encourage them to examine the pictures closely and use the information in them.
- Have the students check their answers by looking at the corresponding page in the Student Book. If you are doing the activity in class, an option is to read the complete conversation aloud or play it on cassette so that students can check their answers aurally before looking in their books.

The exercises in the **Write** section reinforce the structures taught in the Study frames. Students should do these exercises after completing the corresponding Practice section in the Student Book. In this new edition, the Write section has been expanded so that all of the structures are thoroughly practiced in the Workbook. The Teacher's Edition lists the Write activities that correlate with each Study frame and Practice section.

- Before assigning the exercises, you may wish to present the example to the class and check for comprehension. You also may want to refer students to the corresponding Study frame and briefly review the structure.

The **Read** section provides students with additional practice in this important skill. After they have completed the corresponding Read section in the Student Book, students should read the Workbook Read passage silently and complete the comprehension exercises that follow.

- Have the student read the passage at home. Encourage them to guess the meaning of any new words from the context.
- Then have the students read the questions and scan the passage again for the answers.

The **Word Game** and **Vocabulary in Context** sections review the new vocabulary with attention focused on meaning. The Word Game can be done by students individually as a writing practice or in groups as a competition. In the Vocabulary in Context activities, students choose one of the words on the right to complete in writing one of the sentences on the left. Selection is based on the meaning of each sentence within the group, as each group of sentences constitutes a unified context.

- Before assigning Vocabulary in Context, you may wish to go over the example. To do this, have the students read the first group of sentences and the words on the right. Make certain the students understand that all answers must make sense within the given context.
- Have the students complete the sentences, either in class or at home. If this is an in-class activity, you may wish to call on individual students to read aloud the completed groups of sentences.

Finally, a **Composition** is included in each unit of this new edition, so that students can practice the important skill of writing. The compositions move gradually from controlled to less controlled, and models or guidelines are provided. Students should write their compositions after completing the Think and Speak section in the Student Book. They are encouraged to write about themselves and topics of personal interest.

- Have the students spend a few minutes reading the instructions and model composition or guidelines before you assign the activity. Answer any questions they may have.
- The compositions may be assigned as homework, but they also make an excellent in-class activity. When the students have completed their compositions, encourage them to read over what they have written and revise as necessary. Revising is an essential part of the writing process, and you may wish to have the students work in groups to improve their compositions.
- If time permits, ask individual students to share their compositions with the class.

The students can correct their own work if the teacher gives them the answers orally or writes them on the board. Another option is to have the students exchange workbooks for correction and then return them to the original owners for checking. To maintain student motivation and monitor performance, it is also necessary that the teacher check the workbooks occasionally.

The workbook exercises reinforce the students' understanding of English and expand the variety of situations in which students learn to use the language. The combination of textbooks, cassettes, and workbooks give the students a wide range of experience in learning English. Hopefully, the new features will make the workbooks even more effective for promoting learning.

Robert Lado
*Washington, D.C.*

# COMPLETE

**Complete the conversation.  Look at pages 1-3 in the Student Book to check your answers.**

JASON: Excuse _me_. Aren't you the people _____ moved into the Wilson's old

_____?

WOMAN: Yes, we are.

JASON: ____ Jason Shell. I live in the blue house _____ the street from yours.

WOMAN: *(Extending her hand)* I'm Lois Hu. How do you ____?

JASON: *(Shaking her hand)* _____ do you do?

MAN: And I'm Steve Hu. *(Shaking Jason's hand)* _____ to meet you.

JASON: Nice ____ meet you, _____. When _____ you move in?

STEVE: _____ Friday.

JASON: I _____ someone might have moved in, _____ I saw a car in the driveway when I got _____ from work. But then I didn't _____ any lights Friday evening.

LOIS: We must have been at the _____ center.

JASON: You know, my _____ and I gave a _____ Friday night. ____ we'd known that you'd _____ in, we would have invited you.

STEVE: That _____ have been nice.

JASON: And you could have _____ some people from the _____. Well, here comes the _____. It's been nice talking to _____.

STEVE: (*Shaking Jason's hand*) I hope we'll _____ you again soon.

LOIS: (*Shaking Jason's hand*) Yes, me, too. In _____, why don't you and your wife come over for _____ tonight?

JASON: Thank you. I'd _____ to, and I'm sure my wife would, too, _____ she's made other _____. I'll stop by right after _____ and let you know for sure.

STEVE: Great. See you _____.

LOIS: Good-bye, now.

JASON: Have a _____ day.

# WRITE

**A. Make statements using past contrary-to-fact conditions for each question and answer below.**

1. Why didn't you go out on Sunday? Because I felt tired.

   *If I hadn't felt tired, I would have gone out last Sunday.*

2. Why didn't you call me last week? Because I lost your phone number.

   _____

3. Why didn't Lois take the job? Because they didn't offer her enough money.

   _____

4. Why did Yoshi take a semester off from college? Because he had to work full-time.

   _____

5. Why didn't the Shells invite the Hus to their party? Because they didn't know the Hus had moved in.

   _____

6. Why did Elaine get to work late? Because she didn't get up on time.

   _____

7. Why didn't you meet us at the restaurant? Because I got lost.

   _____

8. Why did the singer cancel his concert? Because he had a bad cold.

   _____

9. Why didn't Maria pass her exam? Because she didn't study enough.

   _____

10. Why didn't my manager get a promotion? Because she lost an important client.

    _____

**B. Write comments on each of the situations below using *could have*, *should have*, or *shouldn't have*, as indicated in parentheses.**

1. Lydia hurt her back carrying a heavy box by herself. (shouldn't have)

   *She shouldn't have carried it by herself.*

2. Gloria didn't have a good time at the beach because the sun was too hot for her. She had a sun hat in her bag. (could have)

   _____

3. Hong stayed up until 3:00 A.M. and was so exhausted this morning that he could hardly work. (shouldn't have)

   _____

4. Yasser had a lot of free time last week, but he didn't do all his work. (should have)

   _____

5. Sandra did not enjoy herself at the party, but she stayed late. Her friends left earlier. (could have)

   _____

**C. Answer the questions using the cues in parentheses and *might* or *might have*.**

1. Where are my shoes? (under the bed)

   *They might be under the bed.*

2. When did Mary decide to go to law school? (after she served on a jury)

   _____

3. When is Anne coming back to the office? (today)

   _____

4. Where did Yasser learn English? (in school)

   _____

5. Where did I leave my keys? (on the kitchen table)

   _____

**D. Write a probable explanation for each of the situations using _must_ or _must have_.**

1. What's John doing here? I thought he'd gone skiing. Look! His leg is broken.

   _He must have broken it while he was skiing._

2. What happened to the meat I left on the table? No one was home all day ... except the dog.

   _____

3. Look! Julio is asleep. How could he fall asleep during such an interesting movie?

   _____

4. Ling was upset. She was only wearing one earring.

   _____

5. Tong is smiling. He has his term paper in his hand.

   _____

6. Elaine hasn't called for weeks. I can't understand why. We had a little argument when we last spoke to each other, but I didn't think it was anything serious.

   _____

**E. Complete the following sentences according to your own experiences.**

1. _I go to the dentist twice a year_
   whether or not I want to.

2. _____
   if I had a day off.

3. _____
   whether or not I have enough money.

4. _____
   unless it rains.

5. _____
   whether or not I feel like it.

6. _____
   if I have enough time this weekend.

# READ

**Read the following passage. Then check the box next to the correct answer.**

Nasrettin Hoca

Most countries around the world can boast of the wisdom of their own local folk poet or humorist. These humorists are able to teach conventional wisdom through simple stories, fables, or witticisms. In Greece there was Aesop, famous for "Aesop's fables"; in the United States there was Benjamin Franklin, author of *Poor Richard's Almanac*; and in Turkey was the famous Nasrettin Hoca.

Hoca was born in the small village of Horto in central Turkey in 1209 A.D.. He was educated in the Turkish tradition and later served as a "qadi" or judge. He became a favorite in the court of the Sultan (the Turkish "king") and his fame soon spread to all parts of the Turkish world.

Today his stories are told from the Balkans, to North Africa, to the Middle East to Central Asia -- every region touched by Turkish influence. People from all walks of life from the urban intellectual to the village farmer still commonly use his stories to illustrate a point or prove an argument. His humor remains relevant after more than 700 years and thousands of miles, and is truly universal. Here are a few examples:

**Flour for an old rope**. A neighbor asked the Hoca for a rope to hang out the wash. Knowing that he would never get it back, the Hoca replied,

"I'm very sorry, but I'm just going to spread some flour on it."

"Hoca," the neighbor asked in amazement, "who would spread flour on a rope?"

"Whoever does not want to lend it," replied the Hoca.

**The center of the world**. A friend asked Nasrettin Hoca,
> "Tell me, where's the center of the world?"
> The Hoca got up and replied seriously, "Precisely under my right foot."
> "How do you know that?" said the friend.
> "Figure it out for yourself if you don't believe me," answered the Hoca.

**Curiosity**. "Look, Hoca," a friend said, "a whole tray of baklava (a delicious Turkish sweet) is being carried through the street."
> "It's no concern of mine," he replied.
> "But it's being taken to your house," the friend said.
> "Then it's no concern of yours."

The following are a few proverbs attributed to Nasrettin Hoca.

- A sword is not lent during a quarrel. (*Don't give an enemy the means to destroy you.*)

- Who owns a horse? Its rider, just as you own the sword you wield. (*You are responsible for the damage you do, just as you are responsible for the direction your horse goes.*)

- Strong vinegar eats into its jar. (*Bitterness can destroy a person from within.*)

- A body ages, a heart does not. (*People feel the full range of human emotion at any age.*)

- The liar's candle goes out at dusk. (*A person can only lie for so long before he or she gets lost in the lie.*)

1. Folk poets or humorists _____.
   - [ ] a. are also authors
   - [ ] b. relay conventional wisdom
   - [ ] c. are all from Turkey

2. Nasrettin Hoca is known _____.
   - [ ] a. only in Turkey
   - [ ] b. all around the world
   - [ ] c. in regions touched by Turkish influence

3. In "Curiosity," the friend _____.
   - [ ] a. was interested in the baklava
   - [ ] b. did not like baklava
   - [ ] c. wanted to make baklava

# WORD GAME

**A.** Try to find the nine words hidden in the box below and write them in the blanks on the right. They are all the second part of phrasal verbs beginning with *get*. Find them by reading forward, backward, up, down, or diagonally. They are always in a straight line, with no letter omitted. The first word has been circled to give you a start.

get _____          *get across*          _____

```
H  A  I  N  T  O  B
E  G  Y  U  R  G  A
F  B  U  D  N  I  H
A  C  R  O  S  S  E
H  M  L  W  R  O  A
T  A  O  N  I  H  D
N  O  F  F  O  U  T
```

_____     _____

_____     _____

_____     _____

_____

**B.** Now complete the sentences below, using an appropriate phrasal verb with *get* from your list above.

1. I talked for two hours, but it was impossible to ___*get*___ anything *across* to him.

2. Ralph and Ophelia are on vacation, but they have enough money to _____ for two more weeks.

3. They worked on Saturday to _____ with the project.

4. Hurry up and _____ the car. If we don't leave now, we'll run into a lot of traffic.

5. Steve and Lois _____ financial trouble by making a bad investment. They just can't seem to _____.

6. To reach that address, you have to _____ this train.

7. Take it for three stops and _____ at 14th Street; then walk two blocks east.

8. Hong, _____ of bed. It's already 8:00 and you can't be late for school again.

9. When the weather is rainy and cold, it really _____ me _____.

**8**

# VOCABULARY IN CONTEXT

**A.** **Alice and her brother Victor are talking about their upcoming family reunion. Complete the following dialogue between them using the correct forms of the following expressions:** *had better, ought to, would rather.*

ALICE: If you don't go the family reunion, Mom and Dad will be furious. You
_____ not give them any excuses.

VICTOR: I know I should go. I _____ start getting ready right now,
but I _____ go out with my friends.

ALICE: It doesn't matter what you _____ do. Everyone is
expecting you to be at the reunion. You really _____ go.

VICTOR: Yes. I suppose you're right. I _____ go or everyone will be
disappointed in me.

**B.** **Complete the sentences using the correct form of the phrasal verbs below.**

| | | | |
|---|---|---|---|
| get across | get along with | get on | get down |
| get ahead | get into | get off | get out of |
| get through with | get by | get in | |

1. It's a pleasure to *get through with* your work and have some free time.

2. It isn't easy to _____ an idea to someone who isn't listening.

3. Don't let one difficult day _____ you _____.

4. It's usually a waste of time and energy to _____ an argument
about things that can't be changed.

5. The Diazes are well-liked in the neighborhood. They _____ all of
their neighbors.

6. Most of us find that if we want to _____ at work, there's little time
left for play.

7. When prices are high, you can hardly _____, even with a raise.

8. You should tell the taxi driver your destination as soon as you _____.

9. Usually you have to pay your fare right after you _____ the bus.

10. Your legs may feel strange after you _____ a horse.

11. When there's a fire, the fire fighters do their best to help people to
_____ the building as quickly as possible.

# COMPOSITION

**A. A good paragraph usually contains a topic sentence (a sentence which states the main idea of the paragraph), some supporting sentences (examples, facts, opinions, statistics, etc.), and a conclusion. In the following paragraphs, identify the topic sentence by writing TS in the space between parentheses, the supporting sentences by writing SS, and the conclusion by writing C.**

1.  In these modern times we are used to a fast-paced life. (TS) We speed on highways that never end, or take planes to travel even faster. (   ) We eat in fast-food restaurants to save time. (   ) We build machines to do our work as fast as possible, so that we can enjoy more leisure time. (   ) As a result, we are impatient because things move too slowly in our leisure time. (   )

2.  Anthropologists believe that dance developed as part of early cultural rituals. (   ) There were special dances to mark a birth, a marriage, or a death. (   ) Some dances accompanied the planting and harvesting of crops. (   ) Other dances served to praise the gods and to ask them to bring good fortune to the people. (   ) Even though most of these ritualistic dances have disappeared with the rise of modern civilization, dancing itself still remains popular throughout the world. (   )

**B. On a separate sheet of paper, write a short paragraph according the specifications given below. Begin with the topic sentence provided, and add supporting sentences and a conclusion.**

TOPIC SENTENCE: *There are advantages and disadvantages to living in the city.*

SUPPORTING SENTENCES: Name two advantages and two disadvantages.

CONCLUSION: Explain why, in the end, you do or do not like living in the city.

# COMPLETE

**Complete the conversation. Look at pages 21-23 in the Student Book to check your answers.**

WOZZECK: What's all this _about_, Harry?

HARRY: I've got an _____ I want you to open.

WOZZECK: That's what the _____ have been telling me.

ROXANNA: *He* doesn't _____ there's a pearl in the oyster, _____.

WOZZECK: Of _____ not! What foolishness!

CLAY: _____ a *big* pearl in it.

WOZZECK: O.K., give me the oyster. I'll _____ it. Expert watch repairer to open an

_____!

HARRY: How much is a _____ pearl worth, Louis?

WOZZECK: Oh, a hundred. Two _____, maybe.

HARRY: A _____ big one?

WOZZECK: Three, _____.

WRITER: I've _____ at that oyster, and I'd like to _____ it. How much do you want _____ it?

CLAY: I don't know.

WRITER: How about three _____ dollars?

GREELEY: Three hundred _____?

CLAY: Is it _____ right, Mr. Van Dusen?

HARRY: Sure, it's all _____.

CLAY: But suppose there ain't a _____ in it?

WRITER: There *is*, though.

WOZZECK: Don't you _____ to open it first?

WRITER: No. I want the _____ thing. I don't think the pearl's _____ growing.

CLAY: He _____ there *is* a pearl in the oyster, Mr. Van Dusen.

HARRY: I think _____ is, too, Clay; so why don't you just ____ on home and give the money to your _____.

CLAY: Well ... I *knew* I was _____ to find something good _____!

WOZZECK: Three hundred _____! How do you _____ there's a pearl in it?

WRITER: As far as I'm concerned, the whole things's a _____.

# WRITE

**A. Write requests for the following situations. Refer to pages 25-26 in the Student Book for a review of the different types of requests. There may be more than one answer for each item.**

1. Walter and Katia are talking on the phone long distance. Walter is coming to Katia's city soon, and she wants him to give her a call when he arrives. She says, *"Do give me a call when you arrive."*

2. The teacher walks into the classroom. None of the students are in their seats and they're all making noise. She says, _____

3. The teacher is angry because one student just won't stop talking. She finally says, _____

4. Katherine suggests she and her husband George go to the movies, so she says, _____

5. A man and his dog stop in front of a store and the man leaves the dog outside by the entrance. Before going in the store, he says to the dog, _____

6. There's a loud party going on in Tom's apartment. Somebody rings the doorbell, but Tom is too far from the door to open it. He calls out, _____

7. Mary has met some nice people, and she is trying to persuade them to come and visit her some time. She says, _____

8. Mrs. Rodriguez has just arrived at the doctor's office for an appointment. The doctor is not ready for her yet, so the receptionist wants her to wait in the reception area. She says politely, _____

**B. Answer the questions using reflexive pronouns.**

1. Who paid for you at the restaurant?

   *I paid for myself.*

2. Who did she buy those flowers for?

   _____

3. Who does Carlos work for?

   _____

4. Who are you and Alicia making that cake for?

   _____

5. Who taught your children to play chess?

   _____

6. Who dresses your son for school in the morning?

   _____

**C. Complete the sentences using the appropriate reflexive pronouns.**

1. If you want a job to be well done, you sometimes have to do it ___*yourself*___ .
2. I _____ don't know when he'll be arriving, but someone else probably does.
3. The house _____ is very large, but the garden is small.
4. I can't convince Hiroko to come along. Could you talk to her _____?
5. I know you could use some help with this, but there's a lot you two could do _____ to speed up the work.
6. Deborah built that table _____.
7. Carlos wanted to send his assistant over to help us, but I asked if he could come _____.
8. We couldn't find anyone to fix the plumbing, so we had to do the whole job _____.

**14**

# READ

**Read the following passage. Then check the box next to the correct answer.**

## Folk Music

Music has always been an expression of our universal hopes and fears. Perhaps the oldest and purest form of this expression occurs in folk music. It is an unwritten record of the beliefs and attitudes of a culture, passed on by word of mouth. In a sophisticated culture, music is usually written down and does not have to be performed to be remembered. It may be rediscovered after its composer has died. But in a society that lacks a written history, music must be passed directly from one generation to the next.

The songs which survive are probably the people's favorites. Of course, a folk song which we hear today is not exactly the same as the one our ancestors heard. It has changed through interpretations of successive generations.

Each culture develops its own songs which tell tales of heroic leaders, glorious battles, and love. One culture may adopt and change songs from another culture. For example, the same tune may appear as a ballad in Germany and a holiday carol in Poland. It is unlikely that this same tune developed independently in each country. Rather, the people in a border region probably taught it to their friends nearby. Or perhaps it was transferred from area to area by a wandering minstrel, as was common during the Middle Ages in Europe. If the people in another country like the melody of a song but not the theme, they will often adopt the tune and replace the original words or story with something more suitable.

Dance music is one of the most common forms of folk music. The oldest dances developed as part of the rituals all cultures once practiced. These included dances to celebrate birth, marriage, and death, and dances to accompany the planting and harvesting of crops. Though many of these original dances have disappeared, dancing remains popular throughout the world. Yet the dances of different nations are similar in many ways. For example, sword dances are performed in Scotland, England, central Europe, and India. In some countries these probably developed independently; in other countries, such as Scotland and England, they are probably an example of cultural transfer.

Although music students often argue about the original source of a particular folk song, this information is usually unknown. It is agreed, however, that a song is usually the product of one individual who is able to express his or her people's attitudes and feelings through music. Occasionally, a style of music may develop through group efforts. In some African societies, for example, antiphony, or alternation between groups, each singing one phrase at a time, resulted in the development of a distinct musical style.

Forms of music and dance have developed in every culture around the world. Though each culture may add its own flavor to the art, dance and music are truly universals of human behavior.

1. Folk songs have been preserved mainly through _____.
   - [ ] a. phonograph records
   - [ ] b. memory
   - [ ] c. writing

2. The songs which are passed from generation to generation are _____.
   - [ ] a. the ones people prefer
   - [ ] b. the ones with new interpretations
   - [ ] c. the ones that have not changed

3. Dance music was first developed _____.
   - [ ] a. in cultures centered in cities
   - [ ] b. for use with rituals
   - [ ] c. with the rise of modern civilization

4. Music students believe that most folk songs are created by _____.
   - [ ] a. one person
   - [ ] b. groups of people
   - [ ] c. several villages

# WORD GAME

Match the words in the left and right columns to make new words or expressions. The two words will form either a single word, a hyphenated word, or a two-word expression. In some cases, the word in one column can combine with more than one word from the other column. Write the word(s) in the blanks.

1. drive     _driveway_     shell

2. shopping     _____     agent

3. get     _____     way

4. watch     _____     maker

5. space     _____     center

6. egg     _____     craft

7. business     _____     trip

8. sales     _____     together

9. area     _____     release

10. public     _____     relations

11. ticket     _____     code

12. press     _____     clerk

# VOCABULARY IN CONTEXT

**A. Martha is trying to get her car fixed at a local garage. Complete the dialogue below between Martha and her mechanic using the correct forms of the following expressions: *have got to*, *be supposed to*, and *be able to*.**

MARTHA: How soon do you think you'll _____ finish fixing my car?

MECHANIC: I really don't know. The boss tells me what to do, and I _____ work on that truck first.

MARTHA: Do you think I'll _____ drive my car home tonight?

MECHANIC: My boss always tells me to be careful about what I tell people. I _____ not _____ make any promises to our customers. But I think so.

MARTHA: Great! Could I use your phone? I _____ call my husband and let him know.

MECHANIC: I _____ not _____ let anyone use the phone, but go ahead.

MARTHA: Thanks.

**B. Complete the sentences using the correct forms of the phrasal verbs below.**

|  |  |  |
|---|---|---|
| call up | call off | call on |
| call back | call out | call for |

1. The baseball officials had to _____*call off*_____ the game because of rain.

2. It was a long trip to the hospital, but she decided to _____ her friend's mother, who was sick.

3. John stood at the window and _____ to his friend on the street.

4. The recipe _____ equal amounts of sugar and fruit.

5. It's pleasant to _____ friends who are too far away to visit.

6. If you get a message that someone telephoned while you were out, it's polite to _____ as soon as possible.

# COMPOSITION

A. A good paragraph must have unity. To achieve this unity, the writer should treat only one idea in each paragraph. The main idea is expressed in the topic sentence and is supported by other more specific statements. The following text has two main ideas; it should, therefore, be broken up into two paragraphs. Underline the two main ideas and circle the word that should begin each of the two paragraphs.

> Centuries ago, the Bermuda Islands were known as the "Isles of Devils." Remote, uninhabited, and surrounded by dangerous reefs lying just beneath the surface of the turquoise sea, Bermuda was a navigational menace. Mariners who sailed the trade routes of the Atlantic treated the islands with the same fearsome respect as they treated the plague. There are about 150 small islands which make up Bermuda. The seven largest of them are connected by bridges and causeways. Since the islands are close together, they are called the "Island of Bermuda," as if they were just one island.

B. On a separate sheet of paper, write a short, unified paragraph explaining why you like a movie, TV show, or play you have seen recently. First, identify the movie, show, or play by writing a topic sentence similar to the one below. Then, in several supporting sentences, tell what you liked about it. Finally, give your general evaluation of it in a concluding sentence.

TOPIC SENTENCE: One (movie) I have enjoyed recently is (*Batman*).

# COMPLETE

**Complete the conversation.  Look at pages 42-44 in the Student Book to check your answers.**

REPORTER:   What's some of the _most_ important information _____ received

from the Voyager 2 _____?

SCIENTIST:   Well, for one _____, we now believe it's possible _____ some form

of life could _____ on Europa, _____ is one of Jupiter's moons.

REPORTER:   Why do you think _____ could exist there?

SCIENTIST:   Europa seems to have _____, and water is the major requirement for

life as we _____ it.

REPORTER:   Is water the only _____ between Earth and _____?

SCIENTIST:   Yes. We _____ that Earth and Europa evolved in the _____

way, but because Jupiter dimmed, Europa's development _____.

Jupiter was Europa's _____ source.

REPORTER: What _____ the surface of Europa look _____?

SCIENTIST: In our pictures, it looks like a giant _____ that has been

cracked.

REPORTER: Can you _____ water on Europa's surface?

SCIENTIST: No, but we're fairly _____ that the surface is a crust of _____

about five _____ thick. The _____ covers a global ocean perhaps

sixty miles deep.

REPORTER: How can you be sure _____ water on Europa?

SCIENTIST: We studied the cracks on the _____. As a result, we've

_____ that the ice is thin _____ to break, and _____

that happens, water can _____ through.

REPORTER: _____ is Voyager 2 now?

SCIENTIST: It's _____ leaving our solar system and is _____ for interstellar

space, a totally _____ frontier.

# WRITE

**A. Rewrite these sentences using the passive. Include a *by* phrase if it is essential to the meaning of the sentence.**

1. You should keep meat in the refrigerator.

   *Meat should be kept in the refrigerator.*

2. Earthquakes have struck a number of major cities in the last ten years.

   _____

3. The police catch a lot of criminals in large cities.

   _____

4. You shouldn't throw away furniture and other household items.

   _____

5. You can give these items to various charities.

   _____

**B. Make sentences changing the italicized verbs in the sentences below to the passive with *get*. Follow the model.**

1. I hope the police *catch* the thief.

   *I hope the thief gets caught.*

2. The boss is going to *promote* Tim very soon because he's doing an excellent job.

   _____

3. The waiters will *clear* the tables after the customers leave.

   _____

4. I *ruined* the towel because I left it near the stove and it caught fire.

   _____

5. Someone is always *breaking* the tape player.

   _____

**C. Complete the following sentences appropriately. There are many possible answers.**

1. Many people give up eating desserts so that *they can eat a healthier diet.*

2. Since exercise is important for good health, _____

3. Many people would rather live in the country than in the city because _____

4. I'm saving a little money in the bank every week so that _____

5. Since the weather is so bad today, _____

**D. Write a reasonable consequence for each of the situations below, using the expressions in parentheses.**

1. We were hungry and hadn't eaten all day. (so)
   *So we went to a fast-food restaurant.*

2. Few of the students had studied for the exam. (consequently)
   _____

3. Elaine forgot to set her alarm clock before she went to bed. (because of this)
   _____

4. My friend in Thailand hasn't written or called in five months. (therefore)
   _____

5. Alicia went out in the rain without a raincoat or an umbrella. (as a result)
   _____

6. Computer prices keep going down. (as a result)
   _____

# READ

**Read the following passage. Then check the box next to the correct answer.**

## King Sejong the Sage

The Biography of Buddha printed in 1147 A.D. with movable type using Korean and Chinese characters.

Korea in the mid-fifteenth century was a land of great prosperity and stability. The arts and sciences flourished like never before, and tremendous technological advancements were achieved. Surprisingly, this sudden burst of academic and artistic activity resulted from the efforts of one man -- King Sejong the Sage, ruler of Korea from 1419 A.D. to 1450 A.D.

King Sejong was a highly principled, well educated man who introduced many progressive ideas to Korean society. Perhaps King Sejong's most admired accomplishment was the creation and development of *han'gŭl*, an alphabet which was devised specifically for the Korean language. Sejong intended for his writing system to improve the literacy of the common people, and he called it *hunminchŏngum* (the alphabet of the people). The *han'gŭl* was based on years of phonetic research. The result was an elegant, yet simple system that is still in use today. Even the characters themselves have a certain beauty and simplicity. It is said that an uneducated person can learn to read and write with *han'gŭl* in a matter of hours.

Some of Sejong's other areas of influence included administration, printing, economics, science, music, medical science, and humanistic studies. In order to encourage research in these and other fields, he established the Hall of Talented Scholars (*Chiphyŏnjŏn*). There, promising young academics were given the opportunity and money to develop and explore their areas of interest.

Sejong was dedicated to using technological advancements to improve the quality of life of his people. For one thing, he arranged for several comprehensive works on the latest in Chinese and Korean medicine to be compiled and published. Although the official written language of Korea remained Chinese, Sejong encouraged the publishing of all types of materials -- from literature, to music, to medicine, to astronomy -- in the Korean language to make them accessible to his people. He also worked on developing systems for writing both Korean and Chinese music so that pieces of music could be more widely distributed.

Sejong's concern for the common people also extended to tax reform. He decided that the peasant farmers should only pay a percentage of their yearly income rather than a fixed tax which did not take natural disasters like drought and crop failure into account.

King Sejong was indeed a remarkable man. His own personal achievements in phonetics and the Korean alphabet alone would have been enough to make him noteworthy. However, he did much, much more. As the leader of a nation, he proved an excellent administrator and a strong supporter of his people. He encouraged the development of the sciences, literature, music, and education. Even more important, he attempted to make this knowledge accessible to the people in many ways, including the improvement of movable type and the publishing process. Under his administration, great advances were made in a number of fields, and Korea enjoyed a true "golden age."

1. King Sejong the Sage was _____.
   - [ ] a. poorly educated
   - [ ] b. well educated
   - [ ] c. not interested in education

2. *Han'gŭl* is _____.
   - [ ] a. a language
   - [ ] b. Chinese characters
   - [ ] c. a writing system

3. The common people of Korea _____.
   - [ ] a. benefited under Sejong's rule
   - [ ] b. did not agree with Sejong's policies
   - [ ] c. elected Sejong

4. This "golden age" in Korea was the result of _____.
   - [ ] a. the Chinese
   - [ ] b. Sejong's leadership
   - [ ] c. movable type

# WORD GAME

**A. Read each item below and, based on the context, try to guess the meaning of the words in italics.**

1. The man has good manners. He is very *courteous*.

2. Stop making up *alibis*; you simply must learn to arrive on time.

3. Their *dispute* over politics made it impossible for them to be friends.

4. The true meaning of the speaker's words were *misconstrued* by the audience.

5. Because of the workers' *proficiency*, they were given promotions.

6. His remarks were considered *insulting* by the teacher, so he was asked to leave the class.

7. That child always has an *alert* expression on her face. It is no surprise that she scored highest on the exam.

8. A dinner party is no place for a *monologue*; stop talking so much.

**B. Find a synonym (another word with the same meaning) for each word in the left column from the list on the right. Use the context in part A as a guide. Write your answers in the blanks.**

1. courteous       _polite_                    speech

2. alibi           _____           polite

3. dispute         _____           excuse

4. misconstrue     _____           argument

5. proficiency     _____           misinterpret

6. insulting       _____           attentive

7. alert           _____           skill

8. monologue       _____           offensive

**26**

# VOCABULARY IN CONTEXT

**A. Julia is trying to convince Maurice to go out to the movies with her. Complete the dialogue between them using the correct forms of the following expressions: _how about_, _what about_, _how come_, and _what if_.**

JULIA: Maurice, _____ going to a movie tonight?

MAURICE: I've been tired all day, Julia. _____ tomorrow night instead?

JULIA: _____ you're always so tired? Every time I want to go out, you'd rather stay home.

MAURICE: I really want to go out, but I'm exhausted. _____ I promise that we'll go out tomorrow instead? Would that be O.K.?

JULIA: Sure. That sounds good. It's a date.

**B. Complete the sentences using the correct forms of the phrasal verbs below.**

|  |  |  |
|---|---|---|
| give away | give in | give out |
| give back | give up | give off |

1. The flowers outside their window _give off_ a perfume that filled their room each evening.

2. When you borrow something, try to _____ it _____ promptly.

3. I like to _____ anything I haven't used or worn for two years.

4. Maurice knew he had lost the game, so he decided to _____.

5. When Pedro realized that his own plan wouldn't work, he knew that he'd have to _____ to his boss's suggestions.

6. Julia stayed in the bicycle race until her energy _____.

7. After Rosa won the lottery, she decided to _____ many of her possessions to the poor.

8. Hong forgot to take out the garbage yesterday and now it's _____ a bad odor.

9. Mr. Diaz wanted to _____ the gardening tools he had borrowed from Mr. Murphy, but the Murphys weren't home.

# COMPOSITION

A. Newspaper articles can be constructed in many different ways, but most articles begin with a paragraph which answers the questions *who*, *what*, *where*, and *when*. The paragraphs are usually very short so that people can read the article very quickly. Notice that in the article below, the first paragraph gives a summary of the main facts. The second two paragraphs give supporting, explanatory details.

---

Bridgeport, May 1 - Two Bridgeport residents called the police early this morning to report a prowler lurking close to their homes.

Alice Bodin, the first of the callers, said she had been awakened around 3:00 A.M. by a noise coming from behind the garage, which is located near her bedroom window. John Strand called fifteen minutes later to report that he had been awakened by the screams of his son, who thought he had heard someone attempting to enter the back door of the house. Strand lives next door to the Bodin residence.

A police investigation showed that the large garbage containers at both homes had been overturned, and that several other homes on the small street had been similarly attacked. Police speculated that raccoons from the nearby woods may have come to the neighborhood looking for food.

---

B. Find a news item that interests you and, on a separate sheet of paper, write it up as a short news article following the format above. The first paragraph should include answers to the following questions: What happened? Who was involved? Where did it happen? When did it happen? The second and third paragraphs should present supporting details.

# COMPLETE

**Complete the conversation. Look at pages 62-64 in the Student Book to check your answers.**

AGENT: Transcontinental Airlines. _May_ I help you?

DOLORES: I'd _____ to make a reservation on a _____ to Washington, D.C., on the morning ____ March 10th.

AGENT: There's a _____ at 8:30 and one ____ 11:00.

DOLORES: The 11:00 flight _____ be better.

AGENT: And _____ will you be _____?

DOLORES: ____ March 15th. I'd _____ an afternoon flight, if _____. I have a meeting in Washington _____ morning.

AGENT: _____ a flight at 3:15.

DOLORES: That'll be _____.

AGENT: Your name, _____?

DOLORES: Dolores Andersson. That's D-o-l-o-r-e-s and Andersson with _____ s's.

AGENT: Thank _____. You have confirmed _____ for March 10th on Transcontinental flight number 241 _____ Chicago at 11:00 A.M. and _____ in Washington at 1:55 P.M. You are _____ confirmed on _____ flight number 242 _____ Washington on March 15th at 3:15 P.M. and arriving in Chicago at 4:15 P.M. The round trip _____ will be $326. How would _____ like to pay for your tickets, Ms. Andersson?

DOLORES: ____ credit card.

AGENT: Fine. May I _____ your billing address?

DOLORES: The _____ is 1436 Halsted Street, Chicago 60610.

AGENT: _____ your card number?

DOLORES: It's 6710-121740-72409.

AGENT: Would you like to _____ up your tickets at the _____ or would you like us to _____ them to you?

DOLORES: Mail _____, please.

*(At the airport in Washington, Dolores claims her suitcase and asks a skycap for information.)*

SKYCAP: Can I _____ you?

DOLORES: Yes. _____ can I find ground transportation?

SKYCAP: Right _____ there. You can take a taxi, a _____, or the Metro.

# WRITE

**A. Complete the paragraphs with correct pronouns. Choose from *I*, *me*, *he*, *him*, and *we*.**

I was waiting in the rain for a taxi when a car pulled up. I heard a voice ask _Me_ where _____ was going. At first _____ didn't recognize the voice, but then _____ realized it was my friend Carlos.

_____ replied that _____ was going to a meeting downtown, and asked _____ if he could take _____. Carlos told _____ that _____ could and _____ were soon on our way.

Carlos said that _____ hadn't seen _____ for a long time. I told _____ that _____ had been very busy. _____ asked _____ if _____ would like to have dinner with _____ the next night, but I had to refuse.

I told _____ that _____ would call _____ that evening. _____ did, and _____ went to dinner later that week.

**B. Read the following account of a conversation between Tong and Jane. Then write it in dialogue form.**

Tong asked Jane if she liked to dance. She said that she didn't know how to dance very well. Tong said that he would teach her. Jane replied that it wouldn't be easy. Tong asked her if she had a stereo. Jane said yes, but that it was old. Tong said he would come over Tuesday night.

TONG: *"Do you like to dance, Jane?"* _____

JANE: _____

TONG: _____

JANE: _____

TONG: _____

JANE: _____

TONG: _____

**C.** **Write sentences expressing a wish about the phrase in italics. Be sure to use the correct verb tense.**

1. I can't get that job because *I don't speak Chinese.*

   *I wish I spoke Chinese.*

2. It's raining very hard, and *I didn't bring my umbrella!*

   _____

3. *I didn't go to see the movie* because I didn't have time.

   _____

4. *I don't know how to swim,* so I can't go on that boating trip.

   _____

5. I don't like to go to parties because *I'm not a good conversationalist.*

   _____

6. *I can't go away this weekend* because my relatives are coming to visit.

   _____

7. *I can't go to my neighbor's wedding* since I'll be away on a business trip.

   _____

8. *I don't know how to cook,* so I can't make dinner for my friends.

   _____

9. I can't go home at 5:00 P.M. today because *I didn't finish my work.*

   _____

10. There wasn't enough money in my company's budget, so *I'm not going to the business convention in Lima, Peru.*

    _____

11. Carlos didn't come boating with us because *I didn't have time to call him.*

    _____

12. I can't go to Cancun with my friends because *I don't have enough money.*

    _____

# READ

**Read the following passage. Then check the box next to the correct answer.**

## Building Physical Stamina

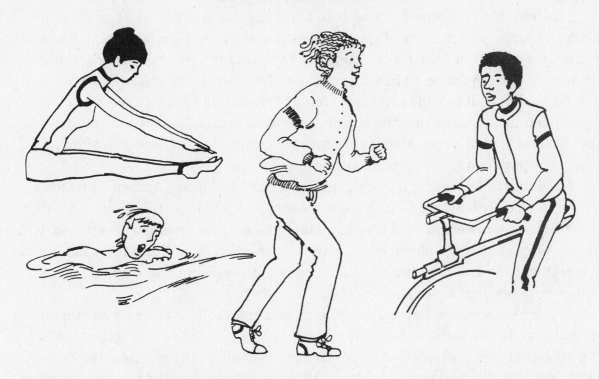

Everyone should be concerned about physical fitness -- everyone, that is, who wants to live a long, active life. Fitness doesn't mean pure physical strength like the kind needed to lift weights. It means overall good health. Physically fit people are free from disease, and have muscles and joints in good working order. But more important, they have "physical stamina," the ability to be active for long periods of time without great fatigue. Stamina depends on strong cardiovascular (heart and vessel) and pulmonary (lung) systems. Fortunately, it is the one aspect of physical fitness over which we have the most control. A person can develop stamina simply through regular exercise.

An understanding of physical stamina depends on a knowledge of body activity. Every movement of the body requires energy. Energy comes from burning fuel -- the food we eat -- by means of the oxygen we breathe in. Food is stored in the body and is used as needed, but oxygen cannot be stored. It must be continuously supplied by breathing. During normal activity, oxygen demands are easily met. But activities such as running, swimming, and prolonged walking demand more oxygen than the lungs can supply with regular breathing. We have all experienced what happens when the body is trying to make up for an oxygen deficit. The chest moves in and out rapidly as the lungs struggle to take in more air. The heart beats fast in order to speed blood (which carries the oxygen) to all parts of the body. The end result is fatigue.

The level of exertion that brings on fatigue is an accurate measure of a person's physical stamina. Almost everyone can perform normal activities without fatigue, but unfit people can become fatigued simply by taking a short walk or climbing a flight of stairs. Their lungs aren't strong enough to take in the necessary oxygen, and their hearts aren't strong enough to pump the oxygen to all parts of the body. Fit people, on the other hand, can withstand a higher level of exertion over a longer period of time.

The best way to conquer fatigue is to build physical stamina by strengthening the heart and lungs; and it is one of the miracles of human physiology that this can be done in a matter of months with proper exercise. Aerobic exercises, those which require large amounts of air, are the best kinds of exercises. Running, swimming, cycling, and long-distance walking all provide aerobic exercise. They demand much more oxygen than normal, but not so much that the activity cannot be maintained for long periods of time. If these activities are practiced regularly with gradual increases in effort, the heart and lungs can reach optimal strength.

Dr. Kenneth Cooper, in the book *Aerobics*, has developed a system by which a person can slowly build stamina. A person accumulates points each week based on the kind of exercise performed and the time spent doing it. The average person can earn enough points to be considered in top physical condition by walking three miles a day in less than forty-five minutes, five times a week; or by swimming a half a mile in about twenty minutes, four times a week.

Aerobic exercise can be free, convenient, and enjoyable. It releases emotional pressures and adds variety to daily activities. As for the need to strengthen the heart and lungs, statistics show the unfortunate results of a lack of exercise. Many cases of heart failure in 40 to 60 year olds results when an activity such as mowing the lawn or shoveling snow puts a sudden strain on the body. It seems that in the long run, the investment of two or three hours a week is well worth the return of added years of living in sound health.

1. A person with stamina always _____.
    - [ ] a. lifts weights
    - [ ] b. has a strong heart and strong lungs
    - [ ] c. is free from disease

2. An oxygen deficit is caused by _____.
    - [ ] a. the heart beating too fast
    - [ ] b. activities requiring extra energy
    - [ ] c. strong lungs

3. Aerobic exercises build the heart and lungs because they _____.

☐ a. require a lot of oxygen

☐ b. can't be maintained for long periods of time

☐ c. require great effort

4. Aerobic exercises are good for _____.

☐ a. straining the body

☐ b. the cardiovascular system

☐ c. heart failure

---

# WORD GAME

**Try to figure out the eight scrambled words below. All of them are key words from the opening conversation on pages 62-64 of the Student Book.**

1. gaebgag _baggage_

2. sdraeds _____

3. cksapy _____

4. piarotr _____

5. oatprntonsarit _____

6. ietvsanrero _____

7. kittec _____

8. tihflg _____

# VOCABULARY IN CONTEXT

**A. Carlos and Martha are planning to attend a business meeting together. Complete the dialogue between them using the correct forms of the following expressions: *as a matter of fact*, *by the way*, and *in any case*.**

MARTHA:  Are you coming to the conference tomorrow?

CARLOS:  Yes, I am. _____ Martha, are you going to attend that board meeting tonight?

MARTHA:  Yes, _____, I am. Why do you ask?

CARLOS:  I don't want to miss anything, but I may have to leave early.

MARTHA:  Don't worry. I'll tell you all about it and, _____, you can always look at my notes from the meeting.

CARLOS:  _____ I was hoping you'd say that! Thanks!

**B. Complete the sentences using the correct forms of the phrasal verbs below.**

| | | | |
|---|---|---|---|
| go along with | go back | go down | go on with |
| go away | go by | go into | go up |

1. Last summer my parents hoped to ____*go away*____ for two weeks, but they had too much work to do at home.

2. If my parents took a summer vacation each year, they would always _____ _____ to the same place.

3. We decided that we'd rather _____ the group than go by ourselves.

4. The police officer told him that there had been an accident, but she didn't want to _____ detail about it on the phone.

5. They wanted him to _____ the story so that they could hear how it ended.

6. The price of cars continues to _____.

7. I love to sit in a city park and watch all the people _____.

8. When the temperature _____, everyone dresses warmly and moves quickly.

# COMPOSITION

Mr. and Mrs. No are a Korean couple who spent the summer traveling in South America. In Rio de Janeiro they had a small mishap. Fortunately, a young boy named Faustino was able to help them. On a separate sheet of paper, write a paragraph telling what happened based on the picture sequence below. Use the past tense throughout and indirect speech whenever appropriate.

# COMPLETE

**Complete the conversation. Look at pages 81-83 in the Student Book to check your answers.**

SALESPERSON: May I _help_ you?

ANTON: Yes. I'd like to _____ a small radio that picks up _____

from abroad.

SALESPERSON: Then you _____ would want a shortwave _____.

ANTON: Yes, _____ I want to hear _____ programs, too.

SALESPERSON: O.K. We _____ this portable _____ with all _____ bands,

AM, FM, and shortwave.

ANTON: It's nice. _____ you put it on shortwave so I can _____ it?

SALESPERSON: Sure. But you _____ really get good shortwave reception

_____ the store during _____ day.

ANTON: How _____ does it cost?

SALESPERSON: It's on _____ for $149. It was $199.

RAJA: That's _____ than you wanted to _____, isn't it? I _____ you wanted a small _____.

ANTON: I guess you're _____. Do you have anything _____, and ... _____ expensive?

SALESPERSON: Yes. We have _____ one. Good quality. _____ bands. Guaranteed for a year. The _____ is $49.50.

ANTON: That's just about _____ I had in mind. Can I _____ it?

SALESPERSON: _____. Let's plug ___ in. There. This knob is _____ tone.

ANTON: _____ very much for your help. I'm _____ to check a few other stores _____ I buy.

# WRITE

**A. Using the cues, write sentences with the present perfect progressive and *for* or *since*.**

1. Anton/pay taxes/1988

   *Anton has been paying taxes since 1988.*

2. the campers/hike/ten days

   _____

3. Maria/study computers/last month

   _____

4. Raja/take the bus to work/two years

   _____

5. Ana/study yoga/her trip to India last year

   _____


**B. Rewrite the sentences using *when* and the past perfect progressive.**

1. The dog barked for a long time, and then his owner fed him.

   *The dog had been barking for a long time when his owner fed him.*

2. The fire burned for hours, and then the fire fighters arrived.

   _____

3. Mr. Perez was planning to go to Indonesia, and then his company asked him to go to Brazil.

   _____

4. We sat in the restaurant for an hour, and then our lunch was finally served.

   _____

5. Hong was shopping for a shirt, but then he saw a beautiful tie.

   _____

**C. Fill in the tag questions and short answers in the following excerpt from the TV program "Guess My Occupation."**

FIRST PANELIST: You work outdoors, *don't you* ?

GUEST: In a way.

FIRST PANELIST: If it were sunny while you were working, you would get burned,

_____?

GUEST: No, _____.


SECOND PANELIST: Hmmm. You use special equipment in your work, _____?

GUEST: Yes, _____.

SECOND PANELIST: You need special training for your work, _____?

GUEST: Yes, _____.

SECOND PANELIST: Your work is dangerous, _____?

GUEST: Sometimes.


SECOND PANELIST: You're an astronaut, _____?

GUEST: No, _____?

FIRST PANELIST: I've seen your picture in the newspapers, _____?

GUEST: No, _____.

SECOND PANELIST: We give up.

GUEST: I fooled you, _____? I'm a deep sea diver.

# READ

Read the following passage. Then check the box next to the correct answer.

Advertising Then and Now

A.     Advertising is the tool that has always been used to convince the public to buy products. In the beginning, it was a basic and crude tool. Craftsmen cried out to passersby, telling the virtues of their wares. As time passed, advertising became more refined and sophisticated. Today, newspapers, magazines, radio, and television use a variety of means to introduce the public to the many products developed through technology.

Advertising probably began when people started producing a surplus of goods which they could offer to one another. In ancient times, advertising was done orally. Public criers announced information about articles for sale along with news of current events.

The Romans started using recorded advertisements. They smoothed and whitened areas on a wall where advertisements could be written or carved, and sculptors lettered and illustrated stone or terra cotta tablets advertising various goods and services.

In the Middle Ages, people continued to use verbal announcements and written messages, but the new form of advertising, using symbols, was developed as well. Shops displayed a special symbol to indicate what goods or services could be found inside. The striped barber's pole, for example, advertised that the man in the shop would shave your beard, cut your hair, pull your teeth, and perform minor surgery.

The Industrial Revolution caused an explosion in the advertising field. The abundance of luxury goods, coming both from new inventions and from trade with different parts of the world, meant that consumers had to be told more about products than ever before. They had to be persuaded that they needed all these new products and that one product was superior to its many competitors. In addition, new inventions made it possible to duplicate advertisements in quantity. The buying public was soon being exposed to endless amounts of advertising.

1. The first written advertisements appeared _____.
   - ☐ a. in Roman times
   - ☐ b. in the Middle Ages
   - ☐ c. during the Industrial Revolution

2. The striped barber's pole is an example of _____ advertising.
   - ☐ a. oral
   - ☐ b. symbolic
   - ☐ c. written

3. During the Industrial Revolution, advertising _____.
   - ☐ a. became widespread
   - ☐ b. was primarily oral
   - ☐ c. was superior to today's advertising

B.    Advertising soon became a professional business, the job of specialists who pooled their efforts in advertising agencies. Agencies analyzed the market for a product, selected the proper media (newspapers, magazines, etc.) in which to advertise, and wrote and designed advertisements. They began to get involved not only in the creation of advertising, but also in the creation of new products, new markets, and even new consumer needs.

In the 1920s, scientific developments had a great influence on the field. Advertisers stopped believing that products would sell themselves and started to back their efforts with scientific methods instead. Agencies conducted both market and consumer research. They systematically investigated all the factors in selling, the aspects of the product, the character and mood of prospective buyers, the buyers' geographic location, and the buyers' purchasing power.

Since that time, advertising has attracted a lot of criticism because of two questionable techniques. First, advertisers often exaggerate the virtues of a product. Products too often are not what they are advertised to be. Second, advertisers often try to create a need for a product in the minds of consumers when no need exists in reality.

Despite these criticisms, advertising continues to catch the eye of the consumer, who continues to buy. Motivations research seeks to explain why people buy the things they do. Researchers have observed that in a "buying situation," people often act emotionally and impulsively. They react subconsciously to the images and designs on the packaging of a product. Their subconscious directs their actions in a number of ways. For example, they may be willing to pay up to $7.00 or more for a facial cream, but not more than $1.00 for a bar of soap. They buy under the illusion that the facial cream will improve their appearance while the soap will simply make them clean. Modern advertisers realize that their task is to find images which have an emotional appeal for consumers.

Advertising has come a long way since the stone carvings in ancient Rome, but the basic point -- to sell a product -- remains the same. The nature of the products and the philosophy of advertising have changed, however. Ancient advertising tried simply to give information about those products that were necessities of life. Today, advertising aims to sell both necessities and luxury products and to reach the largest number of people possible. Persuasion is the tool of the trade and the key to its success.

1.  A new aspect of advertising in modern times is _____.
    - [ ] a. writing and designing advertisements
    - [ ] b. analyzing the market
    - [ ] c. using persuasion

2.  Advertising agencies have been criticized for _____.
    - [ ] a. false advertising
    - [ ] b. creating new products
    - [ ] c. conducting consumer research

3.  Research shows that today's consumers often base their decisions on _____.
    - [ ] a. the emotional appeal of the packaging
    - [ ] b. motivational research
    - [ ] c. criticism of advertisements

# WORD GAME

**A. Name at least seven fruits containing the letter _a_.**

_apple_

**B. List the five months of the year containing the letter _m_.**

_September_

**C. Think of at least six major cities containing the letter _o_.**

_New York_
_Hong Kong_

# VOCABULARY IN CONTEXT

A. **Patricia and her friend Michael are talking about their plans for summer vacations. Complete the dialogue between them using the correct forms of the following expressions:** *just the same*, *on second thought*, **and** *to tell you the truth*.

PATRICIA: Where are you going on your vacation this summer?

MICHAEL: _____, I haven't really given it much

thought. Maybe I'll go to Cancun. _____, I

don't think I can afford to go anywhere.

PATRICIA: Everyone needs a vacation.

MICHAEL: _____, if I worry about money the whole

time, it won't be a vacation anyway.

B. **Complete the sentences using the correct forms of the phrasal verbs below.**

| put on | put out | put away |
|--------|---------|----------|
| put up with | put off | put down |

1. It's not good to ___*put off*___ a job that has to be done.

2. The first warm day of spring they _____ all their winter clothing.

3. He could hardly wait to _____ his new summer suit.

4. Her parents told her to _____ her fork while she was talking.

5. The teacher wouldn't _____ bad behavior.

6. Many accidents could be avoided if people carefully _____ the fires in their fireplaces.

7. I just can't _____ the unprofessional attitude in my office.

8. The first thing Martha did when she got home from her business trip was to unpack her suitcase and _____ her clothes.

9. Ralph was reading a good detective story and just couldn't _____ the book _____ until he finished it.

# COMPOSITION

**Look at the following vacation ads and choose one that appeals to you. Then, on a separate sheet of paper, write a short, unified paragraph telling why you selected that trip. Before you begin to write, review the information on paragraph structure given in the Composition sections of Units 1 and 2 on pages 10 and 19. Use the specifications provided below to help construct your paragraph.**

TOPIC SENTENCE: *I would really enjoy taking the vacation to (Hawaii) that was advertised by (Island Tours).*

SUPPORTING SENTENCE: Tell what features of the trip make it attractive to you.

CONCLUSION: Summarize your feelings about taking this trip.

## Greece

See ancient Greek ruins in Athens
Travel to the famed Greek Isles
Cruise the blue waters of the Aegean

### 5 days/6 nights
### Only $859!

Includes airfare from New York, hotel and transfers

## Plato Tours
1–800–555–6784

*Call now! Space is limited!*

## H A W A I I

| | | |
|---|---|---|
| MAUI | | Lowest Prices! |
| | | 23 Years in |
| OAHU | *15 DAYS FROM* | Business! |
| | **$1399** | Over Half a |
| KAUAI | Complete | Million Happy |
| | | Customers! |
| HAWAII | | Fully Escorted! |

### ISLAND TOURS
Call for free brochure

## 1 - 8 0 0 - 5 5 5 - 9 0 0 0

# COMPLETE

**Complete the conversation. Look at pages 99-101 in the Student Book to check your answers.**

LYDIA: I saw your _ad_ in the paper and would _____ to apply for a position

in public relations. Here's my application and my _____.

INTERVIEWER: What _____ have you had?

LYDIA: I've _____ as a ticket agent _____ an airline _____ three years.

INTERVIEWER: How is that related to _____ relations?

LYDIA: _____, there's a _____ of public contact involved. I have to _____

to our customers _____ we've overbooked a _____ and can't

take all the _____ with confirmed reservations. Is that

ever _____!

INTERVIEWER: I _____ imagine. So how do you _____ a situation like that?

LYDIA: I _____ that overbooking is _____ on certain _____. I tell the customers we will _____ another flight and provide free meals.

INTERVIEWER: How relieved they _____ be! But this job is a bit _____. It calls for _____ press releases and giving tours to _____ that visit our company.

LYDIA: I can write _____. I had to write all the _____ to customers myself. And don't _____ think my experience _____ customers at the airline would be helpful in _____ work dealing _____ the public?

INTERVIEWER: Well, _____ we provide specific _____ relations training for applicants _____ are well qualified otherwise. Why do you want to leave the _____?

LYDIA: I like _____ for the airline, but the _____ is low and the opportunities for advancement are _____.

INTERVIEWER: Starting salaries aren't very high here _____, but there are _____ opportunities to advance ____ you work hard. Thank you _____ coming in, Ms. Lopez. We'll let you know _____ your application in about two _____.

# WRITE

**A. Rewrite these statements as exclamations with *what* or *how*. Use *what* if a noun phrase is italicized and *how* if an adjective is italicized.**

1. This is *an excellent camera.*

   *What an excellent camera!*

2. The photograph is *beautiful.*

   _____

3. Carlos took us to *a fancy restaurant.*

   _____

4. The food was *wonderful.*

   _____

5. That's *a beautiful rose.*

   _____

6. It smells *nice.*

   _____

**B. Complete these sentences with the appropriate negative auxiliaries.**

1. *Can't* you go to the bank during your lunch? Yes. I think I can.

2. _____ Alicia have taken the wrong train? I suppose she could have.

3. _____ the island of Martinique a part of France? Yes. I'm sure it is.

4. _____ Daniel finished cleaning out the garage yet? No, he hasn't.

5. _____ we lock the door before we leave? I guess we should.

6. _____ we had a wonderful time? Yes, we have.

7. _____ the little boy spill the milk if he serves himself? Of course he won't.

8. _____ I need to move if I took that job? Yes, you would.

**C. Change these statements to negative exclamations.**

1. This has been a pleasant evening.

   *Hasn't this been a pleasant evening!*

2. It was nice of the Hus to invite us to the movie.

   _____

3. That movie was interesting.

   _____

4. That actress is beautiful.

   _____

5. It would be fun to go again next week.

   _____

6. The Hus are a very nice couple.

   _____

# READ

**Read the following passage. Then check the box next to the correct answer.**

Jazz

Jazz is everything from ragtime to mambo, including blues, boogie-woogie, bop, Dixieland, and the music of the big-name swing bands. It is a soulful music that seems to come directly from the heart of the musician, and since it is created through improvisation, it is made anew each time it is played or sung and is often not recorded on paper.

The origins of jazz may be found in a number of places -- along the New Orleans riverbanks, in the chain gangs and minstrel shows of the American South, in the Caribbean Islands, or in Africa.

Jazz is a special kind of music. Its distinguishing features belong to jazz alone. A simple analysis of blues, a style of jazz with all these elements, will clearly show just how special this music is.

The melody in blues, as in all Western music, is based on scales. But in blues, the familiar major scale is modified in the melody so that three notes are always flatted: the E, G, and B become E flat, G flat, and B flat. While the main melody of a blues piece is built on these "blue notes," the harmony of the piece retains the unflatted notes. Your ear quickly picks up this collision of blue notes and regular notes. The result is a dissonant sound, one that you aren't quite comfortable with. It's as though the music is reaching for a note that lies somewhere between the two.

Blues is also characterized by a distinctive rhythm. When the music begins, you feel the steady pulsating rhythm of a 2-beat or 4-beat bar in the background. It's the heartbeat of the music, marked by the beating of a drum, the plucking of a bass, or pressure on a piano pedal. Then the melody of the song comes in. The rhythm of the tune in unexpected. The accents seem out of place. You won't find them on the first beat in a 4-beat bar, but rather on the second or third beat. ONE, two, three, four becomes one, TWO, three, four. This irregular accenting is called syncopation. Carried to the extreme, syncopation can even cause the first beat to disappear completely: ONE, two, three, four becomes ___, TWO, three, four. There are many variations of this rhythm, but all are marked by some kind of syncopation.

So far, we have discussed the structure of jazz -- the rhythm and melody, both of which you can record on paper. But the final element of jazz, the tonal color, is something harder to define. Tonal color refers to the quality of the musical sounds. Straight tones vibrate. Clear notes shimmer or slide. A mute is added to a trumpet or to a trombone, and pure tones become growls and rasps. Even new and different sounds are added to the music. Bongo drums bring a hollow, thumping sound. Maracas add the sound of dried beans in a hollow gourd. Brushes whisper along the top of a snare drum. Cymbals, Cuban cowbells, and other instruments add their color to the music.

All this, the melody, rhythm, and tonal color, creates the setting for the star of the jazz band, the soloist. The jazz soloist hears this "arrangement" of the piece and proceeds from there to make it his or her own. The soloist begins with the melody of his solo part, and launches into an intricate embellishment. He or she improvises by playing the tune with ornaments, figurations, and flourishes of all sorts. The soloist is showing off his or her musical skill, intuitive feeling for the music, and creativity.

1. Most jazz is _____.
   ☐ a. created by improvisation
   ☐ b. recorded on paper
   ☐ c. created by swing bands

2. One of the places jazz originated is _____.
   ☐ a. Europe
   ☐ b. the southern United States
   ☐ c. South America

3. "Blue notes" form part of _____.
   ☐ a. the melody
   ☐ b. the familiar major scale
   ☐ c. the harmony

(continued on page 54)

4. Syncopation comes from _____.
   ☐ a. a very steady rhythm
   ☐ b. the disappearance of the rhythm
   ☐ c. moving the accent to a different beat

5. Tonal color depends on _____.
   ☐ a. the types of instruments used
   ☐ b. how well a musician plays an instrument
   ☐ c. the loudness of the music

6. The jazz soloist must _____.
   ☐ a. make the music his or her own
   ☐ b. create the melody
   ☐ c. sing the melody

## WORD GAME

**Try to form as many words as you can from the letters in the two words below. Proper nouns and plural forms of the same word do not count.**

public relations

*boat*
*point*

# VOCABULARY IN CONTEXT

**A. John and Ophelia are talking about their future careers. Complete the dialogue between them using the correct forms of the following expressions: *keep in mind*, *make up one's mind*, *change one's mind*, *have a heart-to-heart talk with*, *not have the heart to*, and *have one's heart set on*.**

JOHN: I don't know what to do, Ophelia. My mother _____

_____ my becoming a doctor, just like her. I do _____

_____ tell her that I'm not interested in medicine. What should I

do?

OPHELIA: Have you _____ yet about what you really

want to study?

JOHN: Well, I may still _____, but I'm pretty sure

I'd like to study engineering.

OPHELIA: Well, _____ that your mother wants the

best for you. Why don't you _____ your

mother and tell her exactly how you feel? I'm sure she'll listen.

JOHN: That's a good idea. I'd better talk to her now, before I _____

_____. Thanks, Ophelia.

**B. Complete the sentences using the correct forms of the phrasal verbs below.**

> turn down      turn into      turn on      turn over
> turn in        turn off      turn out      turn up

1. When the water boiled, I _*turned off*_ the gas.

2. At the end of the story the thief _____ to be the detective's son.

3. The children loved the story of the caterpillar that _____ a butterfly.

4. When the baby was three months old, she learned how to _____ from one side to the other.

5. The teacher told the students to _____ their papers in an hour.

6. It was getting too dark to read, so I _____ the light.

7. She asked him to _____ the radio because she couldn't hear it.

8. He asked her to _____ the music because it was too loud.

# COMPOSITION

A. Read the newspaper ad below. Then, on a separate sheet of paper, prepare a letter of application to send to Mr. Bowen. Your letter should consist of three paragraphs -- the introduction, the body, and the conclusion. Follow the outline provided.

Times - March 5, 1992

## HELP WANTED

**FLIGHT ATTENDANTS**
Airline seeks male and female employees to train and work as flight attendants on international flights. Applicants should be bilingual, have a neat appearance, and enjoy travel and people. Send applications to:

Mr. Frank Bowen
Intercontinental Airlines
10 Park Avenue
New York, NY 10016

INTRODUCTION
- Express your desire to apply for the job.
- Mention how you learned of the position.

BODY
- Describe your qualifications and related experience.

CONCLUSION
- Tell him that you look forward to hearing from him.
- Tell him you would like to have the opportunity to interview with him.

# COMPLETE

**Complete the conversation. Look at pages 119-121 in the Student Book to check your answers.**

JOHN: You're always __*telling*__ jokes. Are you sending _____ of them to the

joke-writing _____ in the paper?

JULIA: I'll tell you _____, if you _____ not to use it.

ALFRED: O.K. (*John nods in agreement*), we promise. _____ is it?

JULIA: _____ is tough, but what can you _____ count on?

JOHN: I don't _____. What?

JULIA: Your _____.

ALFRED: (*Laughs*) Did you _____ the one about the man _____ buried his _____

battery _____ the mechanic _____ him it was dead?

JULIA: That's a pretty _____ one. (*Laughs*) John, do you have any good

_____ to tell?

JOHN: No, but I know some _____ sayings. _____ you like to hear one?

JULIA: Sure.

JOHN: "There's _____ wrong with having _____ to say; the trick

is _____ to say it aloud."

ALFRED: (*Laughs*) That one is so _____! I just remembered _____

my brother told me _____: "Learning to drive is easy. ____ when it's green;

stop when it's _____; and slow down _____ your instructor turns white."

(*Julia and John laugh.*)

ALFRED: (*Laughs*) Here's _____ one. A hospital is the _____ where the

night nurse _____ that you wake up to take a sleeping _____.

Isn't that the truth, _____?

(*Julia, John, and Alfred laugh.*)

# WRITE

**A. Write sentences with *always* in the present progressive to show a habitual action. Use the cues in parentheses.**

1. Julio catches colds very often. (forget to wear his coat)

   *Julio is always forgetting to wear his coat.*

2. Jason forgets things easily. (lose umbrella)

   _____

3. Ling loves ice cream. (buy a quart)

   _____

4. Hong is very interested in politics. (read articles in the newspaper)

   _____

5. Carlos loves clean city streets. (pick up papers)

   _____

6. Martha loves sports. (play tennis)

   _____

**B. Complete the sentences in the following news report using the future progressive form of the verbs below.**

meet   leave   join   attend   travel   give   make

The president _*will be leaving*_ for a tour of the Far East on Monday. She _____ on her jet. In Manila she _____ a conference of leaders of Southeast Asian countries and _____ a speech before the assembled group. On Wednesday, the president's family _____ her in Tokyo, the next stop. The first family _____ with the prime minister on Friday. The president _____ stops in Singapore and Kuala Lumpur before returning back to her country on Sunday.

**C. Complete the sentences using the information in italics.**

1. Sometimes I *eat a full breakfast*. Other times I just drink coffee in the morning. But my mother insists that *I eat a full breakfast.*

   _____.

2. Lee usually *practices the piano every day*, but sometimes he misses a day. His teacher prefers that _____

   _____.

3. Lois hasn't *learned to drive a car*, but her husband would like her to. Her husband suggested that _____

   _____.

4. Alicia doesn't *write to a student in a foreign country*, but her friend thinks it's a good idea. Her friend recommends that _____

   _____.

5. Carlos seldom *arrives on time for work*. He's usually twenty minutes late. His boss has decided to do something about it. His boss has demanded that _____

   _____.

6. Unlike Mrs. Diaz, Mr. Diaz likes to *spend more time at their apartment in the city* than at their country place. Mr. Diaz prefers that _____

   _____.

7. Men have to *wear a jacket and tie* when they go the restaurant in the Grand Hotel. The restaurant requires that _____

   _____.

**D. Combine the two sentences as in the model.**

1. The package must arrive tomorrow. It's urgent.

   *It's urgent that the package arrive tomorrow.*

2. The doctor must operate immediately. It's imperative.

   _____

3. Co-workers must cooperate with each other. It's necessary.

   _____

4. You should check the weather report before you go on your trip. It's advisable.

   _____

5. Children must eat a balanced diet. It's essential.

   _____

6. Vegetables should be cooked in very little water for the best flavor. It's important.

   _____

7. Call the office immediately if you are delayed. It's imperative.

   _____

8. The washing instructions should be followed exactly if you want your clothes to last. It's advisable.

   _____

9. Someone might arrive late to the meeting. It's inevitable.

   _____

10. I must call my lawyer. It's urgent.

    _____

11. You should watch the Hus' house while they're away on vacation. It's important.

    _____

**Read the following jokes. Then check the box next to the correct answer.**

## A Few Jokes

A.     A farmer was having difficulty with his horse. He wrestled with the reins to stop the horse and he flapped them wildly to get the horse to start.

"Look," said a friend of the farmer, "why don't you say 'whoa' when you want him to stop and 'giddyap' when you want him to go?"

"Listen to me," said the farmer. "That horse kicked me three years ago and if you think I'm going to go asking him for favors, you're mistaken."

The farmer did not want to say anything to his horse because _____.

☐ a. the horse did not speak English

☐ b. the horse kicked him the last time he made a request

☐ c. the farmer liked to flap wildly at the horse

B.     A traveling show had a knife-throwing act, and Lisa went twice to see the fascinating spectacle. When her friend Jorge told her that he was going, she didn't encourage him.

"Don't, Jorge," she said, "you'll be wasting your money."

"Why's that?"

"He has bad aim. He keeps missing her."

Lisa didn't think Jorge should go to see the act because _____.

☐ a. it was too expensive

☐ b. it was not very exciting

☐ c. the man throwing the knife never hit his assistant

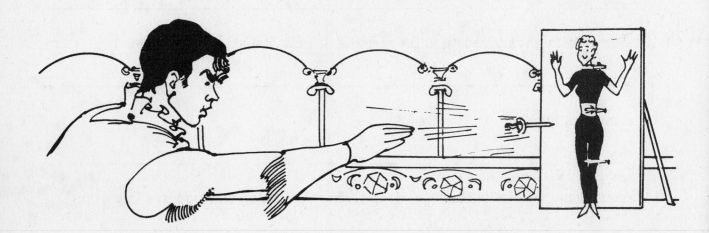

C. The farmer showed the city dweller how to milk the cows and sent him into the fields.

"How many did you milk?" he asked when the city dweller came back.

"Twenty, but there's one thing ..."

"What's that?" the farmer asked.

"I think you should have given me a bucket."

The city dweller _____ back from the fields.

☐ a. brought a bucket

☐ b. brought the milk from twenty cows

☐ c. didn't bring anything

D. Mary's phone rang very early one morning. It was her friend Min and she wanted to know the time.

"It's four o'clock in the morning."

"Thanks," said Min, "I hope I didn't disturb you."

"Not a bit. I had to get up to answer the phone anyway."

Mary had to get up _____.

☐ a. to go to work

☐ b. to answer the phone

☐ c. to find out the time

E. There was a part of the country where the train service was not as good as it should have been. On one occasion a tourist complained about the slowness of the train.

"Why don't you get off and walk?" asked the harassed conductor.

"Because I'm not in that much of a hurry."

The tourist claimed that _____.

☐ a. the conductor was very harassed

☐ b. he should get off and walk

☐ c. walking was faster than taking the train

# WORD GAME

Below are two lists of words. Read the words in the column on the left and then try to match each one with a related word from the column on the right. Look for words which are antonyms or synonyms, or for words which belong to the same categories.

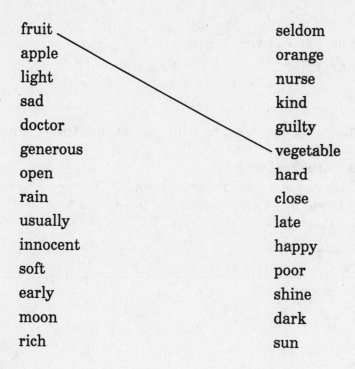

| | |
|---|---|
| fruit | seldom |
| apple | orange |
| light | nurse |
| sad | kind |
| doctor | guilty |
| generous | vegetable |
| open | hard |
| rain | close |
| usually | late |
| innocent | happy |
| soft | poor |
| early | shine |
| moon | dark |
| rich | sun |

# VOCABULARY IN CONTEXT

**A. Lee and his manager Jason are discussing the possibility of buying new computers for their office. Complete the dialogue between them using the correct forms of the following idioms: *over one's head*, *keep one's head*, *go to one's head*, *break one's neck*, and *stick one's neck out*.**

LEE: I can't understand why you don't want to buy new computers for the office.

JASON: I'm sorry, but I think we have to _____ about this. Sure, it would be nice to have new equipment, but the money for it is just not in the budget this year. I'm not going to _____ _____ by ordering computers we can't afford.

LEE: I'm not a manager, so I may be _____ in this matter, but I think you should know the employees' point of view. We _____ every day trying to get our work done on time. A small investment in computers would increase our productivity and morale and save the company money in the long run.

JASON: Actually, Lee, I agree with you completely. But don't let it _____ _____. We're still not going to be able to buy computers this year.

**B. Complete the sentences using the correct forms of the phrasal verbs below.**

| come across | come in | come on | come from |
|---|---|---|---|
| come down with | come off | come over | |

1. At the party he ___*came across*___ an old friend.

2. _____ to my house for coffee tomorrow morning.

3. _____, let's go to the beach.

4. He _____ the South and didn't like the cold winters in New York.

5. After her vacation she _____ a very bad cold.

6. The door to the candy factory opened and the managers invited all the children to _____.

7. A button _____ Joe's coat, and he had to sew it on again.

# COMPOSITION

**A.** The academic year is about to end, and you are planning to take a two-week trip as soon as classes are over. You would like to invite a good friend to go along with you. Write your friend a letter. In the first paragraph, talk about your activities in your final days of classes. In the second paragraph, describe the place you are going to visit. In the third paragraph, try to convince your friend to go with you. The topic sentences are provided for each paragraph.

_____

Dear _____,

    The school year is almost over, and I'm busier than ever. _____

_____

_____

_____

_____

    I'm planning a trip to _____ this summer. They say it's a

fabulous place to visit. _____

_____

_____

_____

    Why don't you come with me? It would be a lot of fun. _____

_____

_____

_____

    Please write back as soon as you can.

                                    Your friend,

                                    _____

# COMPLETE

**Complete the conversation. Look at pages 137-139 in the Student Book to check your answers.**

RALPH: All I _need_ is a good detective _____, and I'm perfectly _____

for the evening. I like a _____ with a fast-moving plot, a book _____

I can't put down until I _____.

OPHELIA: How can you _____ such action-filled trash? There's _____

there. Somebody kills _____ else. The solemn-faced detective

looks for _____ and eventually _____ the killer because it

_____ a perfect _____ after all. No human conflict, ____ character

development, no esthetic experience. _____ bang, bang, you're dead, and

crime doesn't _____.

BETTY: Well, I haven't _____ many detective stories, so I don't _____. But I thought I wouldn't like science fiction _____ I read some really _____ novels by writers _____ Ursula Le Guin and Arthur C. Clarke. I _____ that even when the _____ is outer space, the stories are _____ about human experiences.

RALPH: Science _____ is too complicated for ____. Maybe *you* _____ to speculate about _____ ten thousand years from _____, but I want _____ simple -- the good guys and the bad _____. Besides, you ____ learn a lot about people in a _____ detective story. Everyone has a different _____ for wanting to kill someone. But _____ did it? That's what's _____ for me.

OPHELIA: That _____ be so, but a great novel like Hemingway's *The Sun Also Rises* tells you _____ than who did what. ____ tells you how people's experiences _____ their lives.

BETTY: I don't _____ the subject of a _____ is too important. A good writer can make _____ interesting. It's really the writer's _____ of language that makes a _____ worth reading.

RALPH: Well, it's _____ for me just to find out who _____ the _____ and how the detective figured it out.

# WRITE

**A. Answer the questions using hyphenated modifiers.**

1. What do you call a record that plays a long time?

   *A long-playing record.*

2. What do you call a curve that is shaped like a bell?

   _____

3. What do you call a person who has thin skin?

   _____

4. What do you call a baby with blue eyes?

   _____

5. What do you call an oven that cleans itself?

   _____

6. What do you call a person who moves slowly?

   _____

7. What do you call a factory that is operated by computer?

   _____

8. What do you call a voice with a high pitch?

   _____

9. What do you call a man who educated himself?

   _____

10. What do you call a boat which has been damaged by water?

    _____

11. What do you call a salesperson who talks fast?

    _____

**B. Rewrite these descriptions using hyphenated modifiers.**

1. The earth is a planet shaped like a pear.

   *The earth is a pear-shaped planet.*

2. A hexagon is a figure with six sides.

   _____

3. A horse is an animal with four legs.

   _____

4. Double-knit fabric is a material made by machine.

   _____

5. A "clothes horse" is a person who is dressed well.

   _____

**C. Write a description of the following characters using hyphenated modifiers. Use the information in the chart below.**

JANE: looks funny, talks fast, has a loud mouth, chews gum
AL: looks dangerous, has two faces, talks tough, has a strong will
FRANK: looks ridiculous, has sleepy eyes, has big ears, loves peace
ALICIA: looks beautiful, has brown eyes, has long hair, dresses well

1. Jane is a *funny-looking*, *fast-talking*, *loud-mouthed*, *gum-chewing* woman.

2. Al is a _____, _____,

   _____, _____ man.

3. Frank is a _____, _____,

   _____, _____ guy.

4. Alicia is a _____, _____,

   _____, _____ young lady.

**70**

# READ

**Read the following passage. Then check the box next to the correct answer.**

Pandas

More than 4,000 years ago, the Chinese Emperor Yu paid tribute to a magnificent beast -- a bear-like creature with black markings on its white fur coat. For the next 2,500 years, all reference to this creature vanished, until, in 650 A.D., Chinese manuscripts told of the white bear from the mountainous bamboo forests.

How did this great creature remain hidden for so many centuries? The answer is not so surprising when we read the chronicle of the first Western man who captured a giant panda over 100 years ago. Père Armand David, a French missionary-explorer, set out for the wilds of western China in search of rare plants and animals, including the "great white bear."

The western regions of China were inhospitable to explorers. The panda's home, the almost impenetrable bamboo forests of the rugged mountainsides, was surely the most brutal part of all. Père David, like others before and after him, had to fight the rough terrain, the bitter weathers, and the threat of unfriendly native tribes. These surroundings, however, were well suited to the giant panda. He could live alone comfortably. The bamboo provided a nutritious and steady diet, and its thick growth formed a sturdy shield against the bitter winters.

In 1869, Père David and his men found and captured a giant panda. David might have guessed at some of the attention that the panda would later claim. He realized that the panda had highly unusual physical characteristics and was probably a new species. David wrote that he thought this must be some "new species of bear." In Paris, examiners looked closely at the skins and skeleton and guessed that this "new bear" was not a bear at all, but instead a kind of raccoon.

Although the background and origins of the panda have remained obscure for a long time, the panda's behavior patterns are no longer as mysterious as they once were. Pandas in captivity have given us a clear picture of the character, habits, and tastes of this animal. Because of its size and strength, a panda is a potentially frightful and awesome beast. But its clumsy and uncoordinated ways make him an awkward and defensive creature. It fumbles along, pigeon-toed, in an ungraceful, diagonal walk. He is rarely urged from this lumbering pace. Only a young panda, or a panda in desperate flight, will venture to climb a tree. And once it has reached the top, it has an even greater task to get down.

The panda's personality is also an ironic contrast to its appearance. The panda has been described as shy and timid. Panda watchers at the zoo are often disappointed by the lack of playful spirit in this lovable bear. Water does not tempt it to frolic. In fact, the panda will shy away from bathing as long as possible and then go to great lengths to avoid immersing itself in water. However, many a panda has been seen sleeping contentedly upon a big slab of ice. It is not surprising that this slow-moving and easy-going animal spends most of its time sleeping.

Despite its aloof manner and clumsiness, the giant panda has won a reputation as a loving and adorable creature. With its big, furry head, gentle flat face, and dark-ringed sad eyes, the giant panda is irresistible. Its lopsided movements and its timidity have endeared it to countless friends and admirers at zoos all around the world. But unfortunately for humans, there are so few pandas that the supply cannot meet the demand. Thus, many of us must be content to know them only through representations -- as toy bears, on posters or cards, and in books, cartoons, and films.

1. The first known reference to the giant panda was made _____.
   ☐ a. in 650 A.D.
   ☐ b. By Emperor Yu
   ☐ c. 2,500 years ago

2. The panda was undiscovered for many centuries because _____.
   ☐ a. it is very shy
   ☐ b. its homeland is hard to explore
   ☐ c. no one knew it existed

3. Originally scientists thought _____.
   - [ ] a. the panda was a new species of raccoon
   - [ ] b. the panda was a new species of bear
   - [ ] c. the panda was unrelated to any other species

4. The panda's size and strength _____.
   - [ ] a. make him a dangerous and frightful animal
   - [ ] b. become a handicap by making him awkward
   - [ ] c. helped him ward off hunters and explorers for many centuries

5. Panda watchers at the zoo are often disappointed because _____.
   - [ ] a. the panda walks pigeon-toed at a lumbering pace
   - [ ] b. the panda spends most of its time sleeping
   - [ ] c. the panda is lovable-looking, but lacks a playful spirit

6. The world is fond of pandas because _____.
   - [ ] a. their oversized and awkward shape makes them lovable
   - [ ] b. they are playful and venturesome and responsive to audiences
   - [ ] c. they have rarely been seen in person

## WORD GAME

**A homonym is a word which sounds the same as another word, but has a different spelling. Write a homonym for each word below in the blanks provided. See the example below.**

1. witch  *which*
2. roll  _____
3. add  _____
4. break  _____
5. maid  _____
6. weak  _____
7. stares  _____

8. rode  _____
9. scene  _____
10. site  _____
11. hare  _____
12. plain  _____
13. fair  _____
14. hear  _____

# VOCABULARY IN CONTEXT

**A. Susan and Toshi are talking about a party they recently attended. Complete the dialogue between them using the correct forms of the following idioms:** *by the skin of one's teeth, get on someone's nerves, let one's hair down, and split hairs.*

SUSAN:     I didn't have a good time at John's birthday party at all. It really _____

_____ when people start arguing about politics at a

social gathering.

TOSHI:     I know what you mean. I don't go to a party to _____

_____ . I want to have a good time and _____

_____ .

SUSAN:     I agree. I only managed to stay out of that discussion _____

_____ .


**B. Complete the sentences using the correct form of the phrasal verbs below.**

| | | |
|---|---|---|
| keep away from | keep off | keep out of |
| keep back | keep on | keep up |

1.  "Restrain them, please! _*Keep*_ them

    _*back*_ !" the zoo attendant said to the police

    officer when she saw the crowds who had come to

    see the new baby elephant.

2.  The officer then called out to the visitors: "This

    baby needs to sleep, and it's not good to _____

    him _____ . You must _____

    the fence, and _____ the yard.

3.  He's shy. You'll even have to _____

    the walk surrounding his building because he'll be

    very nervous. But if you _____

    walking up the hill, you'll see him very well from

    there."

# COMPOSITION

**A.   A good composition consists of three parts:**

|  |  |
|---|---|
| INTRODUCTION: | a paragraph or two introducing the topic; |
| SUPPORTING PARAGRAPHS: | several paragraphs dealing with various aspects of the topic; |
| CONCLUSION: | a paragraph summarizing the main points made in the discussion paragraph |

**B.   Reread the story on pages 71-72 about pandas. Use it to write a shorter story of your own about the panda. Write only one introductory paragraph, three discussion paragraphs, and one concluding paragraph. You may use the information from the story or from your own knowledge of pandas.**

**Start by listing your main ideas in the spaces provided. Then write your story on a separate sheet of paper.**

Introduction: _____

_____

_____

Supporting
Paragraph 1: _____

_____

_____

Supporting
Paragraph 2: _____

_____

_____

Supporting
Paragraph 3: _____

_____

_____

Conclusion: _____

_____

_____

# COMPLETE

Complete the conversation. Look at pages 155-157 in the Student Book to check your answers.

CESAR: Hi, Christine! Caroline *said* she saw you _____ the poetry reading

_____ night. Did you enjoy it?

CHRISTINE: Yes. It was one of the best I've _____ attended. The auditorium _____

filled to capacity.

ROGER: _____ poetry did they read?

CHRISTINE: First _____ was a poem by Robert Frost. Then _____ were

several of Emily Dickinson's, and _____ of all were some _____ by

Carl Sandburg. Are you _____ with anything they wrote?

CESAR: _____, I read Robert Frost's "Stopping by Woods on a Snowy Evening"

____ high school.

ROGER: I _____ reading _____ that Emily Dickinson

lived almost _____ a hermit. And furthermore, she was practically

_____ until after her _____.

CHRISTINE: That's right. _____ seven of her poems were _____ during

her lifetime. When she died, they _____ nearly two thousand poems

hidden away in her _____.

ROGER: _____ of Carl Sandburg's poems did they read last night?

CHRISTINE: They read my _____ one, "Chicago."

CESAR: Have you written any poetry _____?

CHRISTINE: Yes. _____ I'd be too embarrassed to let _____ read it ...

CESAR: Oh, come on, Christine. _____ us a few of your poems.

CHRISTINE: Maybe someday I _____. However, if _____ interested in really

good poetry, why _____ you come to the _____ poetry reading?

CESAR: _____ is it?

CHRISTINE: Next Thursday night ____ eight, at the Civic Center. You've _____ to get

there by seven thirty, _____, if you want to get _____ seats.

CESAR: O.K.! I'll come ... How _____ you, Roger?

ROGER: I'll _____ about it and let you know.

# WRITE

**A.** Pablo and Maria have bought paint and are ready to paint their living room. Write some instructions for them by putting the steps below in order and using sequence words such as *first*, *second*, *third*, *next*, *then*, *last*, *finally*, and *last of all*.

remove the furniture
protect the floor
remove the switch plates

stir the paint
clean the walls
paint the walls

*First remove the furniture.*

**B. Divide the sentences below into two. Use the words in parentheses to relate the two ideas. Follow the model.**

1. Young Ho speaks Korean, Japanese, and Thai, and reads Chinese. (in addition)

   *Young Ho speaks Korean, Japanese, and Thai. In addition, he reads Chinese.*

2. Jamal served lamb, chick peas, tomato, and pita bread, and made baklava for dessert. (moreover)

   _____

3. The museum contains paintings, drawings, sculptures, and a wonderful cafeteria. (also)

   _____

4. That letter must be written, typed, stamped, mailed, and at the post office tonight! (furthermore)

   _____

5. I don't like this style, and I refuse to pay more than a hundred dollars for a dress. (moreover)

   _____

6. New York has theaters, interesting buildings, lots of people, and a large park right in the middle. (in addition)

   _____

7. Tonight I have to cook dinner, wash the dishes, iron two shirts, call my mother, feed the dog, and do my homework. (also)

   _____

8. Lucy bought two skirts, a blouse, a belt, and a pair of shoes. (also)

   _____

9. Our history teacher assigned us two chapters from the textbook, three articles, several essays, and a term paper. (moreover)

   _____

**C. Make an opposing comment about these statements. Use the words in parentheses to relate your comments to the statements.**

1. Skiing is a lot of fun. (however)

   *However, it can be dangerous.*

2. Doughnuts are delicious. (but)

   _____

3. Tennis can be an exhausting sport. (nevertheless)

   _____

4. Guayaquil, Ecuador, is very hot. (but)

   _____

5. Instant coffee is convenient. (on the other hand)

   _____

6. Claudia can type very fast. (however)

   _____

7. Pizza originated in Italy. (however)

   _____

8. Haiti is a nice country. (nevertheless)

   _____

9. It takes a long time to become a doctor. (on the other hand)

   _____

10. Latin is a dead language. (however)

   _____

11. The office is usually closed on Saturday. (but)

   _____

12. Computers can increase productivity and save time. (on the other hand)

   _____

# READ

**Read the following passage. Then check the box next to the correct answer.**

## Education in Pre-Columbian Mexico

In the early part of the sixteenth century the Mexica, commonly known as the Aztec, civilization was in its prime. The arts flourished. Engineers were capable of designing and building gigantic pyramids and intricate temples. There was a complicated political structure and an advanced communication network that radiated from the capital, Tenochtitlan (now Mexico City) to both the Pacific and Atlantic coasts. The Mexica empire covered the majority of present day Mexico and included a number of tribes of various cultures who paid taxes to the Mexica confederacy.

In order to maintain a civilization as advanced and as far-flung as the Mexica, it was necessary to develop an educational system which could train young people and pass on the great bodies of knowledge accumulated in the areas of science, astronomy, arts, military strategy, etc. The Mexica system was indeed equal to the task.

Institutional schooling was compulsory for all children regardless of social class. Youngsters usually began their formal education by the ages of six to nine years old. Before that time, their parents were responsible for teaching domestic tasks in the home and for giving good advice about life.

There were two possible educational paths available for Mexica children. One was to attend the *calmecac*, a temple or monastery where they were entrusted to priests and priestesses. The other was the *telpochcalli*, the "house of young men," which was run by experienced warriors. Girls were administered by the *ichpochtlatoque* or "mistresses of young girls." Both boys and girls were educated in either of the two types of schools, but each followed a separate curriculum.

The *calmecac* was typically reserved for the aristocracy, although some children of the trading class and of lower classes were also admitted. There were several *calmecacs* in pre-Columbian Mexico and each was attached to a particular temple. They were strictly administered by priests. The education at the *calmecac* was rigid and severe. Boys endured frequent fasts and hard labor. They drew blood from their legs and ears for penance and ritualistic offerings. Self-sacrifice and self-control were emphasized. In addition to character-building exercises, students were also taught intellectual subjects such as reading and writing in pictographic characters, divination, chronology, poetry, rhetoric, and songs, which were actually documentaries of the history of the Mexica people and chronicles of their wars.

Girls in the *calmecac* were also subjected to rigorous routine. They lived and studied under the direction of elderly priestesses. They learned complex religious rituals and developed their skills in the art of embroidery. Every night they awoke several times to make offerings to the gods.

Things were very different in the *telpochcallis* -- the schools for the common people. *Telpochcallis* were plentiful; there were several in each district. The schools were administered by warriors and the principal aim of the education was to prepare boys for war. They learned how to handle weapons, how to take prisoners, and how to act out military strategy. Of course, they were also taught self-discipline. School boys often went in bands to cut wood for the school or to take part in public works such as the digging of ditches and canals or the cultivating of common lands. At night, though, the boys were given the freedom to sing and dance and enjoy themselves until after midnight. They learned neither the religious ritual nor the intellectual subjects of the *calmecac*.

However, men who had attended the *telpochcalli* were not necessary excluded from high public office. Candidates for certain offices were chosen based on merit alone, not social class or educational background. It was also possible for lower class children of high potential to attend the *calmecac* and thus advance to public office.

Whether at the *calmecac* or the *telpochcalli*, all Mexica children received a formal education which prepared them for productive roles in their society. If the effectiveness of an educational system can be seen as a gauge for the health of a culture, then the Mexica culture certainly seemed poised to live a long and prosperous life.


1.  The Mexica were also known as the _____.
    - ☐ a. *calmecacs*
    - ☐ b. Aztecs
    - ☐ c. Tenochtitlan

2. In the early sixteenth century Mexico _____.
   ☐ a. all Mexica children attended school
   ☐ b. only aristocratic Mexica children attended school
   ☐ c. children were educated only in the home

3. The *calmecacs* were _____.
   ☐ a. run by warriors
   ☐ b. plentiful throughout Mexico
   ☐ c. attached to a particular temple

4. Mexica girls in the *calmecac* _____.
   ☐ a. did not learn anything
   ☐ b. learned complex religious rituals
   ☐ c. became warriors

5. Men who had attended the *telpochcalli* _____.
   ☐ a. could never hold public office
   ☐ b. did not have to work
   ☐ c. could sometimes rise to high public office

---

# WORD GAME

---

**Match the words in Column A with the words in Columns B and C which contain the same vowel sounds.**

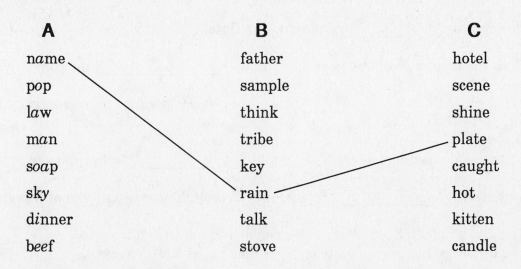

| A | B | C |
|---|---|---|
| name | father | hotel |
| pop | sample | scene |
| law | think | shine |
| man | tribe | plate |
| soap | key | caught |
| sky | rain | hot |
| dinner | talk | kitten |
| beef | stove | candle |

# VOCABULARY IN CONTEXT

**A. Julio's friend Susan wants to buy a car, and Julio is giving her some advice. Complete Julio's statements to Susan below using the correct forms of the following idioms: *catch someone's eye*, *see eye to eye*, *play it by ear*, *pay through the nose*, and *be up to one's ears*.**

"I tried to _____ when I saw you talking to Steve about buying his old car. Steve's car has a lot of miles on it and it's pretty old. You have to be careful or you could end up _____ for something that just isn't worth much. You could _____ in mechanical problems before long. You should just discuss the matter with Steve casually until you both _____ on a fair price. Until then, you shouldn't count on having the car. Just _____.

**B. Complete the sentences using the correct form of the phrasal verb below.**

| | | |
|---|---|---|
| take after | take off | take over |
| take down | take on | take up |
| take in | | |

1. After six hours of studying, my mind was too tired to _*take in*_ any more names and dates.

2. I decided to _____ playing the flute.

3. When the boss retires next year, her son will _____ the company.

4. Carlos couldn't _____ any more projects because he was already too busy.

5. Martha said she'd feel better if she could _____ a few days to rest.

6. If my children _____ me, they'll need glasses by the age of fifteen.

7. After the accident, Susan took out a pencil and paper and tried to _____ the number of the license plate on the other car as it drove away.

# COMPOSITION

**A. Read the sample composition below.**

> My favorite movie is "Out of Africa" starring Meryl Streep and Robert Redford. "Out of Africa" was made in the 1980s and tells the true story of a Danish woman living in Kenya around the time of World War I.
>
> The principle character, Karen Christiansen, marries a Swedish aristocrat, and the two of them move to Africa to start a new life. They live in an English settlement and operate a large coffee farm. During the film, Karen experiences difficult times in both her personal and business relationships. In the end, her farm is destroyed by fire and she is forced to return alone to her native Denmark.
>
> The movie deals with how our experiences and environment affect and change our lives, and how we, in turn, affect and change those around us simply by our presence. Karen's character evolves throughout the film, and she returns to Denmark a very different person than she was when she left. Africa had changed her. And she had changed Africa, too. During her years there she had made an impact on many people and left an impression behind in the minds of those she had known.
>
> "Out of Africa" is a sweeping, epic work filmed in beautiful, natural surroundings. It is a very moving film, and I found it to be both thought-provoking and powerful.

**B. Now, on a separate sheet of paper, write a composition of three or four paragraphs about your favorite book or movie. Use the guidelines below to help you form your composition.**

**Introduction:** Identify the book or movie and its author, director, or star. Then give a brief introduction to your topic.

**Discussion:** Summarize the plot of the book or movie and tell about some of its important features.

**Conclusion:** Describe your reaction to the book or movie. Why do you like it?

# COMPLETE

Complete the conversation.  Look at pages 174-176 in the Student Book to check your answers.

OSCAR:  You _know_, Martha, I constantly _____ to write letters, reports,

_____, notices, and even essays. I _____ now that my

_____ had made me write _____ in college. I just _____ to

sit down and write. ____ other words, I can't put down on _____ what I

think. It _____ comes out scrambled. I _____ even punctuate well.

MARTHA:  That's _____. I think ____ teachers made me write _____ much, even

in my _____ classes. In fact, I spent so much time _____

that I hardly had _____ time to master the subject matter, and that's

_____ counts if you want to _____ an engineer.

OSCAR: But that's _____ all that counts. You'd think that an _____ only _____ to know math, science, and that _____ of thing, but everybody has to _____ letters, take notes, and write _____ and reports of one kind or another. And I _____ it so difficult that I simply _____ it.

MARTHA: But notes and letters are _____ to write. And you can always get _____ to write an occasional report.

OSCAR: _____. Notes and letters are _____ to write. But if you write a note to your _____ and misspell a word, you'll see what _____ to his or her opinion of you. You may be the _____ engineer in the company, but your boss's _____ in you could be shaken.

MARTHA: But you can look up _____ in the dictionary. We all have to do _____ anyway, right?

OSCAR: It's not that simple. For _____, you don't know _____ words you're _____ to misspell, so you either look up _____ word, _____ is totally impractical, or you _____ a few words. And even your best friends won't _____ you about your spelling _____. Besides, if they did, you'd _____ feel embarrassed or resentful.

# WRITE

**A. Rewrite the following groups of sentences in the space provided. Add an introductory expression such as *for instance* or *for example* before the last sentence in each group.**

1. New York is a great city to visit. There's so much to do and see there. You can go to the theater, the ballet, or the opera almost any night of the week.

   *New York is a great city to visit. There's so much to do and see there. For instance, you can go to the theater, the ballet, or the opera almost any night of the week*

2. Politicians are not always genuine. They make promises and then forget them when they are elected to office. Before our mayor was elected, he said he'd improve the schools, but nothing has been done yet.

   _____

   _____

   _____

3. If you want to do something useful for your community, you can always do volunteer work. There are many public institutions which need people to help. You can be a volunteer fire fighter.

   _____

   _____

   _____

4. There are many different ways to make money in your spare time. There are several things you can do in your own home. You can sell magazine subscriptions by telephone.

   _____

   _____

   _____

5. Some communities are making a real effort to beautify their streets. A local neighborhood association has just planted flowers along several blocks.

   _____

   _____

   _____

**B. Rewrite the following groups of sentences in the space provided. Add an introductory expression such as *in short*, *in other words*, or *to summarize* before the last sentence in each group.**

1. My trip to Miami was so relaxing. I went to the beach every day and met some really nice people. I had a marvelous time.

   *My trip to Miami was so relaxing. I went to the beach every day and met some really nice people. In short, I had a marvelous time.*

2. Mr. and Mrs. Diaz get along really well. They rarely have arguments and always make important decisions together. They have a perfect marriage.

   _____

   _____

   _____

3. Maria's husband has been in the hospital for several weeks. She has a family at home to take care of and she has to stay late at the office almost every night. She's under a lot of pressure.

   _____

   _____

   _____

4. The boss is planning a New Year's party at our office. She thinks it's a good opportunity for employees to relax and chat with their co-workers. She believes a party would be good for morale.

   _____

   _____

   _____

5. Tong's party was a lot of fun. I met some new people and the food and music were great. It was a fantastic party.

   _____

   _____

   _____

**Read the following passage. Then check the box next to the correct answer.**

## Space Talks

A.     Imagine this scene -- Alex is chatting with his friend Bill at a restaurant. The small table is set, and two friends are waiting for dinner. It has been a long, exhausting day, and Alex is still trying to relax. Without thinking, he starts to fiddle with the items on the table. First he moves the salt shaker toward Bill. Alex's movement catches Bill's eye, but Bill continues to talk, unbothered. Then Alex begins to rearrange the silverware and the napkins, first his and then Bill's. Now Bill becomes uneasy. He shifts around in his chair and folds his arms in front of him. Nevertheless, the two men keep on with their conversation. Finally, Alex slides the breadbasket along the edge of the table until it is very close to Bill. At this point, Bill becomes very irritated, even though his chat with Alex has been very pleasant. Bill is puzzled by the way he feels, and Alex cannot understand his friend's irritation. How can their behavior be explained?

Anyone listening to Alex and Bill's friendly conversation would suppose that everything was fine. The explanation cannot be found in what Bill or Alex said, but rather, in what they did. Their actions represent a concept that is crucial to our total communication. Alex used his body as an instrument of language. The way his body moved in the space that surrounded them told Bill that Alex was threatening him.

All of us, like Alex and Bill in the story, use space to communicate. As soon as we are born, we begin to relate to the space around us. We claim a bubble of space as our own -- almost feel as if we were staking out territory and defending it, as many animals do. We feel threatened if anyone enters it. In the story, neither Alex nor Bill owned the table in the restaurant, and yet, because it fell into the area of space each had designated as his own, each unconsciously claimed part of it as soon as he sat down. They divided the table into two equal parts; an invisible line formed a barrier between Alex's space and Bill's. When Alex started to move things over onto Bill's "side" of the table, Bill became uneasy. He felt threatened by Alex who, because of his movements, was subconsciously identified as an intruder into Bill's area of space. Even though Bill knew Alex was his friend and he knew that Alex meant no real harm, he was antagonized by Alex's actions.

Each day we encounter situations in which our handling of space plays an important role. Dr. Edward T. Hall, an anthropologist, has developed a science called "proxemics" that describes how people utilize space and how their use of space communicates certain facts and signals to other people. Dr. Hall contends that there are four different "zones" of space that people mark out for themselves. The "public zone" of space is the one which strangers may enter without a person feeling threatened. The "social zone" is the zone where strangers and acquaintances may enter to conduct formal or informal business. The "personal zone" of space is one in which only friends and relatives are welcomed. Finally, a person has an "intimate zone" where only the people that are the very closest to him or her are allowed -- people such as husband or wife, mother or father. We feel uncomfortable in a crowded room when others come too close to our "personal zone" of space. If we bump into someone on a bus, in the street, or anywhere, we excuse ourselves, not so much because we think that we have hurt that person, but because we realize that we have invaded his or her "personal" space.


1. Bill does not become uneasy about what Alex is doing until _____.
   ☐ a. Alex knocks the breadbasket off the table
   ☐ b. Alex moves around in his chair
   ☐ c. Alex moves Bill's silverware and napkin


2. Bill becomes irritated because _____.
   ☐ a. of the way Alex is moving around
   ☐ b. of something Alex said
   ☐ c. Alex has not been very pleasant

3. Like animals, Alex and Bill were unconsciously _____.
   - [ ] a. staking out territory on the table
   - [ ] b. trying to own the restaurant
   - [ ] c. claiming to own the table

4. Proxemics is a science that describes _____.
   - [ ] a. how people threaten each other
   - [ ] b. how people utilize space
   - [ ] c. how people communicate with strangers

B.   What is communicated through the use of space can also vary from one culture to another. People of different cultures have different concepts of what their zones of personal spaces should be. For example, people from northern Europe and the United States may sometimes feel uncomfortable conversing with Arabs or Latin Americans, and vice versa. Northern Europeans and Americans prefer a relatively large distance between speakers while Arabs and Latin Americans are more at ease with closer distances.

   In Japan, where a dense population makes crowded conditions a way of life, it would seem logical to conclude that the Japanese people exhibit no concept of "personal" or "intimate" space. Actually the contrary is true. The Japanese have a very definite idea of space. To them, a person's house is an area of "personal" space, and thus they resent any intrusion into their homes.

   Every culture defines and employs spaces in a slightly different way. For this reason it is important that people of all cultures be aware and try to understand how space can be used to communicate.

1. What is communicated through the use of space is _____.
   - [ ] a. the same for all people
   - [ ] b. different for all people
   - [ ] c. different for different cultures

2. The important thing that we can conclude from this article is that _____.
   - [ ] a. all cultures use space in the same way
   - [ ] b. people must learn how to stand closer together when they are speaking
   - [ ] c. people must learn to understand how they use space to communicate

# WORD GAME

**Below are some lists of related words or themes. Cross out the word that does not belong to the category, and then think of a title for the list.**

### *Animals*

| | | |
|---|---|---|
| cat | bus | artist |
| horse | subway | doctor |
| ~~needle~~ | plane | engineer |
| cow | airport | teacher |
| mouse | car | lawyer |
| dog | bike | medicine |

| | | |
|---|---|---|
| red | yell | play |
| orange | scream | narrative |
| yellow | whisper | essay |
| tan | shout | poem |
| blue | screech | guitar |
| fish | holler | short story |
| brown | bellow | novel |

# VOCABULARY IN CONTEXT

**A.** Ellen and her husband Pablo are discussing a party they are having for some friends. Complete the dialogue between them using the correct forms of the following idioms: *out of hand, put one's foot down, pull one's leg, put one's foot in one's mouth, cost an arm and a leg,* and *have one's hands full.*

ELLEN:     Everything is so disorganized. Things are really getting _____
_____ around here. You know I _____
_____ getting this surprise anniversary party ready for
Alicia and Mark. Well, I have a million things to do. Nothing is ready, and
now you've come in for lunch. I've got to _____
_____ and say, "I just can't do it."

PABLO:     But I didn't come for lunch. I came to tell you that Alicia and Mark are both
sick. It's contagious, but not serious. The doctor says they can't go out.

ELLEN:     Come on, Pablo, you're _____.

PABLO:     No. I'm really serious. In fact, I almost _____
_____ by laughing when Alicia's daughter told me about it. I was
thinking of the party, of course.

ELLEN:     I could cry.

PABLO:     Come on, Ellen, don't let it get you down. It's really quite funny.

ELLEN:     Funny! Do you have any idea what this party has cost us? It's _____
_____.

PABLO:     We can keep the party things, and we'll just eat ice cream and cake for
breakfast, lunch, and dinner for the next three weeks.

**B.** Complete the sentences using the correct forms of the phrasal verbs below.

|  |  |  |
|---|---|---|
| look around | look forward to | look like |
| look down on | look into | look up |

1. My boss said she would _____ *look into* _____ the matter before deciding.

2. Maria is a very nice person, she never _____ anyone.

3. I always use the wrong name when I introduce Lucy to people, because she _____
_____ her cousin Carolina.

4. If you don't understand a word, _____ it _____ in the dictionary.

5. He _____ the party because all his friends would be there.

6. When I'm in a new city, I like to _____ a while before
planning what I want to do.

# COMPOSITION

**A. Read the following poem carefully.**

## Two Kinds of People

There are two kinds of people on earth today,
Just two kinds of people, no more, I say,
Not the good and the bad, for 'tis well understood
The good are half bad and the bad are half good.

Not the happy and sad, for the swift flying years
Bring each man his laughter and each man his tears.
Not the rich and the poor, for to count a man's wealth
You must first know the state of his conscience and health.

Not the humble and proud, for in life's busy span
Who puts on vain airs is not counted a man.
No! The two kinds of people on earth I mean
Are the people who lift, and the people who lean.

Wherever you go you will find the world's masses
Are ever divided in just these two classes.
And, strangely enough, you will find, too, I wean,
There is only one lifter to twenty who lean.

This one question I ask. Are you easing the load
Of overtaxed lifters who toil down the road?
Or are you a leaner who lets others bear
Your portion of worry and labor and care?

Author: Ella Wheeler Wilcox, American poet and novelist
Born: In 1850 in Johnstown Centre, Wisconsin
Died: October 31, 1919, in England

**B. Now, on a separate sheet of paper, write a three-paragraph composition about the poem following the guidelines below.**

INTRODUCTION: Identify the poem and its author and give a brief biographical sketch using the information supplied after the poem.

DISCUSSION: Explain the topic of the poem and the poet's message.

CONCLUSION: Describe your reaction to the poem. Did you like it or dislike it? Why?

# INVENTORY TEST 1

**Check the box next to the correct word or words.**

**Example:** I wish you _____ come to the party.

☐ a. will
☐ b. can
☐ c. could
☐ d. will have

1. My parents insisted that I _____ piano lessons as a child.

☐ a. takes
☐ b. did take
☐ c. take
☐ d. be taking

2. The award _____ tonight.

☐ a. will be given
☐ b. will given
☐ c. be given
☐ d. will give

3. There are a lot of ways to cook fish. _____, you can fry it.

☐ a. On the other hand
☐ b. For example
☐ c. However
☐ d. Finally

4. I'm going to the party _____ I finish my household chores.

☐ a. unless or not
☐ b. whether
☐ c. because
☐ d. whether or not

5. Min is a _____ person.

☐ a. love-fun
☐ b. fun-loving
☐ c. loving-fun
☐ d. fun-love

6. Julie _____ for a car for months when she finally found one.

☐ a. been looking
☐ b. had been look
☐ c. had been looking
☐ d. be looking

7. I _____ more attention in class today.

☐ a. should have paid
☐ b. should have pay
☐ c. have pay
☐ d. did paid

8. _____ a scare I had!

☐ a. How
☐ b. What
☐ c. Which
☐ d. Why

9. I built the house _____.

☐ a. himself
☐ b. myself
☐ c. self
☐ d. my

10. _____ you're hungry, we should stop and eat.
- [ ] a. So that
- [ ] b. So
- [ ] c. Thus
- [ ] d. Since

11. _____ he had left on time, he wouldn't have been late for school.
- [ ] a. When
- [ ] b. Because
- [ ] c. If
- [ ] d. Would

12. Nobuko _____ since nine o'clock.
- [ ] a. has been working
- [ ] b. been working
- [ ] c. working
- [ ] d. be working

13. Shakespeare wrote many wonderful plays. _____, he is known for his poetry.
- [ ] a. Third
- [ ] b. In addition
- [ ] c. Since
- [ ] d. Consequently

14. Rosa made _____ a cup of tea.
- [ ] a. herself
- [ ] b. himself
- [ ] c. themselves
- [ ] d. self

15. Carlos is a _____ man.
- [ ] a. educated
- [ ] b. self-education
- [ ] c. self-educated
- [ ] d. educated-self

16. _____ you heard that Pilar and David are getting married?
- [ ] a. Haven't
- [ ] b. Didn't
- [ ] c. Weren't
- [ ] d. Couldn't

17. Alicia told me that she _____.
- [ ] a. would stay
- [ ] b. stay
- [ ] c. would stayed
- [ ] d. staying

18. _____ answer the phone!
- [ ] a. Let
- [ ] b. Not
- [ ] c. Somebody
- [ ] d. No

19. Did Mr. and Mrs. Perez say that they _____ to come with us?
- [ ] a. have wanted
- [ ] b. will have wanted
- [ ] c. wants
- [ ] d. want

20. Jason's _____ trying something new. Today he's water skiing. Tomorrow he's sky diving.

☐ a. never

☐ b. not

☐ c. always

☐ d. sometimes

21. Some television programs are interesting and educational. _____, most are a waste of time.

☐ a. As a result

☐ b. Consequently

☐ c. However

☐ d. For example

22. I finally _____ after waiting for one hour in the restaurant.

☐ a. serve

☐ b. got

☐ c. get served

☐ d. got served

23. When _____ at the meeting?

☐ a. would you be arrive

☐ b. will you be arrive

☐ c. would you arriving

☐ d. will you be arriving

24. I _____ my credit cards at home.

☐ a. must left

☐ b. must have left

☐ c. will have left

☐ d. have leave

25. Lisa wishes she _____ a rock star.

☐ a. was

☐ b. were

☐ c. would

☐ d. be

26. The movie was boring. _____, many people left before the end.

☐ a. So that

☐ b. Consequently

☐ c. Because

☐ d. Since

27. Carlos is not a _____ man.

☐ a. bad-tempered

☐ b. bad temper

☐ c. bad tempered

☐ d. badtempered

28. _____, you should put a quarter into the machine.

☐ a. Because

☐ b. So that

☐ c. First

☐ d. Since

29. Has he _____ gotten tall!

☐ a. still

☐ b. always

☐ c. constantly

☐ d. ever

30. You're from Peru, _____?

☐ a. isn't you

☐ b. weren't you

☐ c. couldn't you

☐ d. aren't you

31. _____, I think we should all try to please our customers.

☐ a. Because

☐ b. So that

☐ c. Since

☐ d. To summarize

32. It's important that you _____ reservations today.

☐ a. make

☐ b. would make

☐ c. makes

☐ d. making

# REFERENCE KEY FOR INVENTORY TEST 1

**If you missed any items on Inventory Test 1, locate the numbers of the items on the list below and study the corresponding exercises in the Summary and Exercises section.**

| TEST ITEM | EXERCISE NUMBER | TEST ITEM | EXERCISE NUMBER |
|---|---|---|---|
| 1 | 23 | 17 | 13 |
| 2 | 8 | 18 | 5 |
| 3 | 31 | 19 | 12 |
| 4 | 4 | 20 | 21 |
| 5 | 25 | 21 | 30 |
| 6 | 16 | 22 | 9 |
| 7 | 2 | 23 | 22 |
| 8 | 18 | 24 | 3 |
| 9 | 7 | 25 | 14 |
| 10 | 10 | 26 | 11 |
| 11 | 1 | 27 | 27 |
| 12 | 15 | 28 | 28 |
| 13 | 29 | 29 | 20 |
| 14 | 6 | 30 | 17 |
| 15 | 26 | 31 | 32 |
| 16 | 19 | 32 | 24 |

# SUMMARY AND EXERCISES

1. **If** with contrary-to-fact past conditions:
   *If he had left home on time, he wouldn't have been late for school.*

**If** introduces a contrary-to-fact condition in the past. The past perfect tense (**had known, had gone**) is used.

A clause with **would have** indicates willingness to have done the action if the condition had been met.
   *If I had seen you, I would have said hello.*

A clause with **could have** indicates that an opportunity was not taken because the condition was not met.
   *If it hadn't rained, we could have gone to the beach.*

**Exercise 1: Make contrary-to-fact statements using past conditions. Follow the model.**

1. I didn't plan for my vacation, so I didn't save any money.

   *If I had planned for my vacation, I would have saved some money.*

2. I didn't get a raise this year, so I couldn't take a vacation.

   _____

3. I didn't have money for travel, so I couldn't visit my friends in Paris.

   _____

4. I didn't visit my friends in Paris, so I didn't see the Louvre.

   _____

2. **Should have**, **would have**, and **could have** in contrary-to-fact sentences:
   *I should have paid more attention in class today.*

**Should have** refers to an obligation in the past that was not fulfilled.
   *I should have called you yesterday.*

**Would have** refers to a past willingness to do something that was not done because of some other condition.
   *I would have called you if I had remembered.*

**Could have** refers to an unused ability or opportunity in the past.
   *I could have written myself a reminder, but I didn't.*

**Exercise 2: Write an appropriate comment on the following situations using the cues in parentheses.**

1.  John had a bad headache, but he didn't do anything about it. (could have)

    *He could have taken an aspirin.*

2.  Lois didn't feel well, but she went to the party. (should have)

    _____

3.  Jason has a stomachache because he ate the whole pie. (shouldn't have)

    _____

4.  Hong was bored by the TV program, but he continued watching it. (could have)

    _____

    _____

3.  **Must** and **must have** indicating probability and **might** and **might have** indicating possibility:
    *I must have left my credit cards at home.*

**Must** can indicate probability. Use **must** plus the simple form of the verb for the present tense. The past tense consists of **must have** plus the past participle. **Might** and **might have** work like **must** and **must have**, but they refer to possibility.
*You must be tired today since you stayed up so late last night.*
*I might go to Florida if I can save enough money.*

To form the negative, place **not** after **must** or **might**.
*Hong might not have washed the dishes since he had so much homework to do.*

**Must** can also be used in the present tense to indicate obligation, but **must have** plus the past participle only indicates probability.
*I must call my mother today after work.*

**Exercise 3: Mr. and Mrs. Levy are eating breakfast and suddenly realize their son Alex has left for work without his wallet. Complete their conversation below with *must, might, must have*, or *might have*.**

Mrs. Levy:  Look! Here's Alex's wallet. He *must have* forgotten to take it with him this morning. I wonder how he got to work.

Mr. Levy:  I don't know. Maybe he had some money in his pocket. Or he _____ borrowed some money from his friend Jill. They travel together on the train.

Mrs. Levy:  I think he _____ come back for it at lunchtime.

Mr. Levy:  Yes, he _____ . . . if he has time.

4. **If**, **unless**, and **whether or not**:
   *I'm going to the party whether or not I finish my household chores.*

**If** declares that the main idea will happen when the condition happens.
   *If you are late, I'll wait for you.*

**Unless** declares that the main idea will happen except when the condition happens. **Unless** is the same as **if** + **not**.
   *I'll attend the meeting unless I'm still sick.*

**Whether or not** declares that the condition is not necessary for the main idea to happen.
   *The company picnic will be held next Saturday whether or not it rains.*

**Exercise 4: Complete the sentences according to your own experiences.**

1. Whether or not the weather is good, *I walk to school in the morning.*

2. I don't get angry unless _____

   _____

3. If I don't do my homework, _____

   _____

4. I go to class whether or not _____

   _____

5. Unless we stop polluting the earth, _____

   _____

6. I usually feel happy if _____

   _____

## 5. Requests:
*Somebody answer the phone!*

In some request sentences, the subject is expressed to make the request more emphatic.
> *Everybody listen!*
> *You be quiet!*

**Everybody** is used to emphasize that the request applies to every person present. **Anybody** is used in negative requests to emphasize that no one can violate the request. **Somebody** is used to indicate that one person, it doesn't matter *which* person, should fulfill the request. **You** simply makes a request stronger. When the subject of a request is not expressed, **you** is the implied subject.

> *Everybody sit down!*         *Somebody answer the phone!*
> *Don't anybody leave yet!*      *You stop that! = Stop that!*

Sentences beginning with **let's** and **let's not** are requests which include the speaker. **Let's** is the contraction of **let us**.
> *Let's go to Toronto by bus.*      *Let's not take the train.*

Adding **do** to a request makes it more persuasive.
> *Do come and see me again!*      *Do be careful while driving!*

Requests with **no** usually appear on signs. They have the force of a command. Sometimes such a command is softened by the use of **thank you**.
> *No fishing.*                  *Thank you for not smoking.*
> *No parking.*

**Please**, when added to a request, makes it more polite.
> *Please answer the phone!*      *Please don't leave yet.*

**Exercise 5: Complete the sentences below with an appropriate request. There may be more than one answer.**

1. Elaine wants to take a trip to Hawaii with her husband, so she says to him, _"Let's take a trip to Hawaii."_

2. Mr. Hu hears the phone ring while he's in the shower. He shouts to his children, _____

   _____

3. The young students are talking and making a lot of noise in class. The teacher is trying to get them to look at the map. He says, _____

   _____

4. The officials of our local park noticed that people were leaving a lot of garbage behind when they had picnics in the park. So the officials put up signs near the garbage cans which say

   _____

## 6. Reflexive pronouns as objects:
*Rosa made herself a cup of tea.*

Reflexive pronouns combine **my**, **your**, **him**, **her**, or **it** with **-self** in the singular and **our**, **your**, or **them** with **-selves** in the plural.

A reflexive pronoun can be used as a direct object when the direct object is the same as the subject and as an indirect object when the indirect object is the same as the subject. When used as a direct or indirect object, a reflexive pronoun comes immediately after the verb or the verb phrase.

*I bought myself a new bike.*
*The Shells hurt themselves while skiing.*
*The child cut herself on a piece of glass.*

A reflexive pronoun can also be used as the object of a preposition.
*Sometimes people talk to themselves.*

**Exercise 6: Answer the questions using reflexive pronouns.**

1. Who makes dinner for Carlos? _He makes dinner for himself._

2. Who taught Lisa and Laura to skate? _____

3. Who dressed Lily and Paul this morning? _____

4. Who are you and Jaime baking cookies for? _____

5. Who did you buy that new car for? _____

_____

## 7. Reflexive pronouns as emphasizers:
*I built the house myself.*

Reflexive pronouns can be used to give extra emphasis. They emphasize that it is the subject of the sentence, and not someone else, who is responsible for the action. It is not the object of the sentence. It appears either after the subject or at the end of the sentence or clause.

*The officials themselves were not aware of the problem.*
*The officials were not aware of the problem themselves.*

**Exercise 7: Complete the sentences with the correct reflexive pronouns.**

1. Fred ___himself___ was responsible for the evening's success.

2. The music _____ was not outstanding, but the orchestra was superb.

3. The Ayalas planted the whole garden _____.

4. I saw the entire accident _____.

5. You _____ said that the movie was boring.

## 8. Passives:
*The award will be given tonight.*

The passive voice indicates that the subject is the receiver of the action. It is constructed with the appropriate tense of the auxiliary **be** and the past participle of the verb. The object of the corresponding active sentence becomes the subject of the passive one.

*The school principal will give <u>John</u> the award.*
*<u>John</u> will be given the award.*

The subject of the active sentence can be expressed in a **by** phrase.
*<u>Our</u> <u>chairperson</u> will give the award.*
*The award will be given <u>by</u> <u>our</u> <u>chairperson</u>.*

**Exercise 8: Rewrite the sentences below using the passive. Include a *by* phrase only if it is essential to the meaning of the sentence.**

1. Joyce has invited us to the party.

   *We've been invited to the party.*

2. Someone will pay that bill tomorrow.

   _____

3. Picasso did that painting in the 1940s.

   _____

4. You should return all books to the library on time.

   _____

5. Photographers are taking pictures of the president's family.

   _____

6. Rudolph Diesel invented the diesel engine.

   _____

   _____

## 9. Passive with **get**:
*I finally got served after waiting for one hour in the restaurant.*

In informal conversation you can usually use a passive with **get** instead of with **be**. The subject receives the action of the verb.

*Han was invited to the party.*
*Han got invited to the party.*

**Exercise 9: Rewrite the sentences below using the passive with *get*.**

1.  The driver delivered the package to the wrong address.

    *The package got delivered to the wrong address.*

2.  Someone should type this letter soon.

    _____

3.  I hope that they invite us, too.

    _____

4.  If you aren't careful, someone will steal your purse.

    _____

5.  I wore my boots almost every day last winter.

    _____

6.  The photographer in the store took my picture.

    _____

_____

## 10. Cause and purpose subordinators:
*Since you're hungry, we should stop and eat.*

**Since** and **because** indicate cause. **So that** and **so** indicate purpose.
> *The accident occurred because there was ice on the road.*

The order of the cause or purpose clause and the main clause can be changed.
> *I'm going to stay at home tonight since I don't want to miss Linda's phone call.*
> *Since I don't want to miss Linda's phone call, I'm going to stay home tonight.*

**Exercise 10: Complete the following sentences with an appropriate cause or purpose.**

1.  Since the weather's so beautiful today, *I'll go to the park.*

2.  _____ so that my English will improve.

3.  The man was put in jail because _____

4.  Many people exercise so _____

5.  So that we don't lose any more time, _____

6.  Since you'll be out of town all next week, _____

## 11. Sentences related by cause and consequence:
*The movie was boring. Consequently, many people left before the end.*

Use **as a result, because of this, consequently, for this reason, so, therefore,** and **thus** at the beginning of a sentence to indicate that the sentence is a consequence of the preceding one. All but **so** are separated from the rest of the sentence with a comma. **Thus** and **therefore** are generally used in formal speech and writing.

*Our environment is precious. Thus, we should try not to pollute it.*
*Energy is becoming less available. Consequently, energy costs are going up.*
*I haven't saved any money. So I can't afford to go away.*

**Exercise 11: Write original sentences that are reasonable consequences of the situations below using the words in parentheses.**

1. It snowed a lot last night, and all the roads are closed this morning. (as a result)

   *As a result, many businesses and schools are closed.*

2. Mark arrived at the airport and discovered that he had forgotten his passport. (therefore)

   _____

3. When Angela got home from work last night, she felt exhausted. (so)

   _____

4. My cough has been getting worse every day. (consequently)

   _____

5. Computers are being used by more and more businesses. (for this reason)

   _____

_____

## 12. Change of person in indirect speech:
*Did Mr. and Mrs. Perez say that they want to come with us?*

The use of **that** is optional when reporting someone's speech.
*Dolores told me (that) she enjoyed her trip.*

Use **if** or **whether** to report a yes-no question.
*I asked Martha whether she wanted to come to my party.*
*I asked Martha if she wanted to come to my party.*

Use the appropriate question word **where, what, how,** etc. to report an information question. Note that in indirect speech, unlike information questions, the verb follows the subject.
*I asked Dolores where she went on her vacation.*
*I asked her how she traveled there.*

**Exercise 12: Make new sentences using indirect speech. Follow the model.**

1. My father always tells me, "You ought to relax more and go out with your friends."

   _My father always tells me that I ought to relax more and go out with my friends._

2. I answer him, "I can't because I have too much work to do."

   _____

3. He says, "If you work all the time, you'll become exhausted, and nothing will get done."

   _____

4. I tell him, "Maybe you're right."

   _____

5. He says, "People need to balance their work life and their social life in order to enjoy both."

   _____


## 13. Change of tense in indirect speech:
   _Alicia told me that she would stay._

When changing from direct to indirect speech, make the appropriate change of tense. If the verb which introduces the indirect speech is in the past (**said, told, asked**), the main verb or modal in the reported speech also changes to the past.
   _Alicia reported, "I'll be working in Hong Kong."_
   _Alicia reported that she would be working in Hong Kong._

**Exercise 13: Write new sentences using indirect speech. Follow the model.**

1. I asked my teacher, "Can I have more time to do my report?"

   _I asked my teacher if I could have more time to do my report._

2. She said, "I don't need it until next week."

   _____

3. She said, "I'll give the whole class an extension because everyone seems to need more time."

   _____

4. I said, "Everyone is going to be very relieved to hear that."

   _____

## 14. **Wish** + subjunctive:
*Lisa wishes she were a rock star.*

In a sentence with **wish**, the subordinate verb expresses a desired action or state that has not occurred or does not exist. It is contrary to fact. If the desired action or state is in the present, the subordinate verb phrase is in the past.
   *I wish I had some money.*

If the desired action or state is in the past, the subordinate verb phrase is in the past perfect.
   *I wish I could have gone to Portugal with my friends last month.*

**Exercise 14: Write sentences expressing wishes about the italicized phrases.**

1. Unfortunately, *we can't solve the problem of poverty*, and many people continue to live under difficult circumstances.

   *I wish we could solve the problem of poverty.*

2. *I'm not a good singer*; I can't even carry a tune.

   _____

3. *I don't know how to type*, and now I have to type a term paper.

   _____

4. *I can't swim* because I never learned how as a child.

   _____

   _____

## 15. The present perfect progressive:
*Nobuko has been working since nine o'clock.*

The present perfect progressive is formed with **have** or **has** + **been** + the **-ing** form of the verb. It indicates an uninterrupted action that began in the past and is continuing in the present. The fact that the action continues into the present is emphasized.
   *Patricia has been learning Spanish since last summer.*

**Exercise 15: Using the cues, write sentences with the present perfect progressive and *for* or *since*.**

1. Julio/live/in Miami/1990 *Julio has been living in Miami since 1990.*

2. Hong/sleep/ten hours _____

3. The temperature/fall/yesterday _____

4. She/teach/math/four or five years _____

## 16. The past perfect progressive:
*Julie had been looking for a car for months when she finally found one.*

The past perfect progressive is formed with **had been** + the **-ing** form of the verb. It indicates an activity that was in progress before some other action in the past. The fact that the action was in progress in the past is emphasized.

*Manuel had been living in Caracas before he came to Mexico City in 1990.*

**Exercise 16: Rewrite the sentences using the past perfect progressive and the connector *when*. Follow the model.**

1. I drove for five hours, and then I got a flat tire.

   *I had been driving for five hours when I got a flat tire.*

2. Tien worked at that job for five years, and then he got a promotion.

   _____

3. Nabila lived in Morocco for many years, and then she moved to France.

   _____

4. The family looked for their missing dog for several hours, and they finally found him.

   _____

---

## 17. Tag questions:
*You're from Peru, aren't you?*

An affirmative sentence takes a negative tag, and a negative sentence takes an affirmative tag.
*Tong can speak English, can't he?*
*Martha doesn't live around here, does she?*

A tag question with a falling intonation means the speaker expects confirmation of an opinion. The expected answer agrees with the subject and verb in the main sentence.
*It's a beautiful day, isn't it?  Yes, it is.*

A tag question with rising intonation has the same meaning as a yes-no question.
*The movie starts at eight o'clock, doesn't it?  Yes, it does.*

**Exercise 17: Fill in the tag questions and short answers in the conversation below.**

LINDA: You've returned Sylvia's call, *haven't you* ?

ROB: Yes, _____ . She wanted to know about Yoshi. He's arriving tonight,

_____ ?

LINDA: You just spoke to him on the phone, _____ ?

ROB: No, _____ . I wasn't able to reach him. I'll try again later.

## 18. Exclamations with **what** and **how**:
*What a scare I had!*

Exclamations with **what** and **how** indicate that something or someone is remarkable, extraordinary, or unusual. **What** is followed by a noun phrase, and **how** is followed by an adjective.

*What an interesting novel!*
*How fortunate you are!*

**Exercise 18: Rewrite the statements below as exclamations. Use *what* when a noun phrase is italicized, and *how* when an adjective is italicized.**

1. Tom was *foolish*. _How foolish he was!_____

2. This is *a great dinner*. _____

3. You're *smart*. _____

4. The cake smells *delicious*. _____

5. It's *a long meeting*. _____

---

## 19. Negative questions:
*Haven't you heard that Pilar and David are getting married?*

A negative question is formed by adding **-n't** to the auxiliary of the affirmative. A speaker who asks a negative question generally expects an affirmative answer. A negative answer is possible, however.

*Wasn't that movie awful?*
EXPECTED ANSWER: *Yes, it was.*
POSSIBLE ANSWER: *No, it wasn't. I liked it.*

**Exercise 19: Complete the sentences with the appropriate negative auxiliaries.**

1. ___Haven't___ you ever been to the Crazy Horse Café?
   Of course I have.

2. _____ you agree that it's possible?
   I guess I would.

3. _____ he say that he wants to join our group?
   He did indeed.

4. _____ you at the lecture last night?
   I sure was.

5. _____ we have helped that stranded driver?
   You're right. I guess we should have.

## 20. Exclamations with yes-no question form:
*Has he ever gotten tall!*

In exclamations with yes-no question forms, every word is stressed. The intonation is usually high on every word except on an affirmative auxiliary. Sometimes the intonation is extra high on the subject only. The affirmative and negative forms sometimes have the same meaning.
*Aren't you lucky!   =   Are you lucky!*

The word **ever** is often included in affirmative exclamations.
*Are you ever lucky!*

**Exercise 20: Change these statements first to negative exclamations, and then to affirmative exclamations using *ever*.**

1. The wedding was lovely.

   *Wasn't the wedding lovely!*
   *Was the wedding ever lovely!*

2. The reception will be fun.

   _____

   _____

3. There are a lot of people here.

   _____

   _____

4. They're dressed beautifully.

   _____

   _____

## 21. Present progressive for habitual and future reference:
*Jason's always trying something new. Next week he's sky diving.*

The present progressive can express habitual action in the present. It is sometimes used to tell about a bad habit. Frequency expressions such as **always** and **constantly** are used in this case.
*Elaine's always working on her computer.*

The present progressive can also refer to the near future.
*Antonio's arriving sometime this evening.*

The present progressive usually refers to an action of limited duration in progress at the time of speaking.
*My mother is staying with me for the rest of the month.*

**Exercise 21: Using the cues, write sentences with the present progressive.**

1. Maria/always/argue  *Maria's always arguing.*_____

2. My boss/come/to dinner/tonight _____

3. John/constantly/travel _____

4. Next month/I/move/to a new house _____

## 22. Future progressive:
*When will you be arriving at the meeting?*

The future progressive is formed with **will** + the **-ing** form of the main verb. It is often used in formal situations to ask polite questions or in informal situations to start a conversation. It can also be used to talk about actions that will be in progress in the future.
   *How many nights will you be staying at the hotel?*

**Exercise 22: Complete the following conversation using the future progressive form of the verbs below.**

| work | attend | move | do | look for | keep |
|------|--------|------|-----|----------|------|

STEVE: What ___*will*___ you ___*be doing*___ this summer?

JUAN: I _____ a new job. And my wife and I _____
into our new house. What about you?

STEVE: I _____ school all summer, I'm afraid. If I have time, I
_____ part-time as well.

JUAN: It looks like we _____ busy.

---

## 23. Verb tense in subordinated sentences following certain verbs:
*My parents insisted that I take piano lessons as a child.*

The simple form of the verb occurs in subordinated sentences after verbs such as **recommend, insist, propose, demand, prefer, suggest, request, require**, and **urge**.
   *Jim's doctor recommends that he eat healthier foods.*
   *Roslyn suggested that we go dancing.*

**Exercise 23: Complete the sentences in an appropriate manner.**

1. Julie was hungry, so Jack proposed that ___*they go out for dinner.*___

2. Doctors generally recommend that _____

3. Our teacher requires that _____

4. It was past midnight, and Billy's mother insisted that _____
_____

5. Mr. Wong felt ill, and his wife suggested that _____
_____

6. Martha was exhausted after hiking for three hours, so Carlos insisted that _____
_____

## 24. Verb tense in subordinated sentences following certain adjectives:
*It's important that you make reservations today.*

The simple form of the verb occurs in subordinated sentences following adjectives such as **important, necessary, inevitable, urgent, unavoidable, essential, advisable,** and **imperative**.

*It's imperative that you telephone if you're going to be late.*
*It's essential that she learn some Chinese before going to China.*

**Exercise 24: Combine the sentences below as in the model.**

1. We must all work together for peace. It's necessary.

   *It's necessary that we all work together for peace.*

2. The doors should be locked at night. It's important.

   _____

3. You ought to apply for that job. It's advisable.

   _____

4. John should call his father at once. It's essential.

   _____

   _____

## 25. Hyphenated modifiers ending in **-ing**:
*Min is a fun-loving person.*

Hyphenated modifiers can be formed from action verb phrases. To form the modifier, place the verb at the end of the phrase and add **-ing**. The hyphenated modifier is closely joined in speech, and both words are stressed. This joining is indicated in writing by a hyphen (-).

*That was a nerve-shattering experience.*

**Exercise 25: Change the sentences to include hyphenated modifiers.**

1. That's a story that warms the heart. *That's a heart-warming story.*
2. There's a car that looks beautiful. _____
3. That's a vehicle that moves fast. _____
4. This is a drawing that catches the eye. _____
5. This is a cake that tastes great. _____
6. Hung is a boy who works very hard. _____

**114**

## 26. Hyphenated modifiers with past participles:
*Carlos is a self-educated man*.

To form the modifier, place the past participle of the verb at the end of the phrase and place a hyphen between the two words.
*Martin spoke in a low-pitched voice.*

Hyphenated modifiers can also be formed from passive verb phrases.
*All the furniture in the house was water-damaged.*

Reflexive pronouns such as **himself**, **herself**, **themselves**, **yourselves**, **yourself**, and **myself** all become **self** when used in hyphenated modifiers.
*That industry is self-regulating.*

**Exercise 26: Rewrite the sentences below to include hyphenated modifiers.**

1. That's a sweater made by machine. *That's a machine-made sweater.*

2. That's an area that was damaged by hurricane. _____

3. Monique is a woman who has employed herself. _____

4. It's a radio that is operated by battery. _____

5. It was a farewell that was filled with emotion. _____

## 27. Hyphenated modifiers formed from noun phrases:
*Carlos is not a bad-tempered man*.

Hyphenated modifiers can be formed from noun phrases (**right hand, sad face, loud voice**). To form the modifier, add **-ed** to the noun and place a hyphen before it. No verb is involved in the formation of these modifiers.
*The Smiths are kind-hearted people.*
*A cube is a six-sided figure.*

When changing a noun phrase that includes **good** into a hyphenated modifier, **good** sometimes becomes **well**.
*She's a person with good manners.*     *He's a person of good humor.*
*She's a well-mannered person.*         *He's a good-humored person.*

**Exercise 27: Rewrite the sentences below changing the italicized noun phrases into hyphenated modifiers.**

1. Leona is a person with a *strong will*. *She's a strong-willed person.*

2. Lee is a child with a *chubby face*. _____

3. Mr. Chill is considered to be a person with a *cold heart*. _____

4. The Diaz's children have very *good manners*. _____

**115**

## 28. Organizing ideas in sequences of sentences:
*First, you should put a quarter into the machine.*

Use the words **first, second, third, finally,** and **last of all** to organize ideas in a series of sentences containing ideas that are of equal importance. Separate these words from the rest of the sentence with a comma.

*First, Meredith is well-qualified for the job.*
*Second, she is currently attending night school to further her education.*
*Finally, she understands how our company does business.*

Use the words **first, second, third, next, then, finally, last,** and **last of all** to describe the order in which a sequence of activities took place or will take place.

*Second, press the correct button.*
*Next, wait while the machine pours your coffee.*
*Finally, open the plastic door and remove the cup.*

**Exercise 28: Write the instructions for making popcorn by putting the steps in order and using sequence words such as *first, second, third, next, then, last, finally,* and *last of all*.**

| | |
|---|---|
| add the popcorn kernels | let the kernels pop |
| heat the oil | cover the pan |
| put a small amount of oil in a pan | pour melted butter over the popcorn |

*First, put a small amount of oil in a pan.*

_____

_____

_____

_____

_____

_____

## 29. Relating ideas by addition:
*Shakespeare wrote many wonderful plays. In addition, he is known for his poetry.*

Use **also, in addition, moreover,** and **furthermore** at the beginning of the second sentence to indicate that its idea follows the same line of thought as the preceding one.

*The restaurant is inexpensive. Moreover, the food is excellent.*

Separate these phrases from the rest of the sentence by a pause in speaking and a comma in writing.

**Exercise 29: Complete the following sentences with an appropriate idea of your own.**

1. I accomplished a lot today. I finished cleaning out my desk. Furthermore, *I wrote ten letters to my friends.*

2. Exercise is necessary to develop healthy bones. In addition, _____

_____

3. The doctor told Tom to reduce his cholesterol intake and watch his weight. Moreover,

_____

4. My boss wants me to take more initiative in my work. Also, _____

_____

_____

## 30. Relating an idea as an exception or limitation:
*Some television programs are interesting and educational. However, most are a waste of time.*

**But, however, nevertheless**, and **on the other hand** introduce a statement that is in opposition to, or contrasts with, what precedes it. **But** and **however** point out the contrast or opposition.
   *Ayhan's spoken English is perfect. However, his written English needs some work.*

**Nevertheless** and **on the other hand** emphasize the contrast.
   *Flying your own plane can be thrilling. On the other hand, it can also be dangerous.*

When **but** is the first word in a sentence it is not followed by a comma.
   *But I'm going to try it anyway.*

**Exercise 30: Make an opposing comment about these statements. Use the relating words given.**

1. Photography is a fun hobby. But *it can be expensive.*

2. Cookies and cakes taste good. However,_____

3. I don't have a lot of money. Nevertheless,_____

4. Owning a car can be very convenient. On the other hand,_____

_____

5. Getting a university degree takes a lot of time and energy. Nevertheless, _____

_____

## 31. Introducing an example:
*There are a lot of ways to cook fish. For example, you can fry it.*

**For instance** and **for example** introduce an example. They are separated from the rest of the sentence by a pause in speaking and a comma in writing.
   *Bamboo has many uses. For instance, it is often used to make furniture.*

**Exercise 31: Write an example for each statement below using your own information. Begin with *for example* or *for instance*. Either expression is correct in each sentence.**

1.   The countries of the world have many serious problems to solve.

   *For instance, there is world hunger.*

2.   I've done several interesting things this year.

   _____

3.   There are many good ways to practice English.

   _____

   _____

## 32. Introducing a summary or restatement:
*To summarize, I think we should all try to please our customers.*

**In other words, in short,** and **to summarize** are used to introduce a summary or restatement of what has preceded. Such phrases are separated from the rest of the sentence by a pause in speaking and a comma in writing.
   *The lake is beautiful. The weather is lovely. I feel relaxed. In short, everything is perfect.*

**Exercise 32: Write your own summary or restatement of each paragraph.**

1.   The ventilation is my office is poor, and the air is always stale. The bright lights bother my
   eyes, and the furniture is falling apart. In a word, *it's an unpleasant*
   *place to work.*

2.   Clara's essay was well argued and well organized. It was fascinating to read. There were no
   grammar or spelling errors. To summarize, _____

   _____

3.   I think we should hire Boris. He's a responsible employee who has never missed a day of
   work or even arrived late. He takes the initiative in projects, and always completes what he
   has started. In other words, _____

   _____

# INVENTORY TEST 2

**Check the box next to the correct word or words.**

**Example:** The letter _____.

☐ a. been written
☐ b. have been writing
☐ c. has been written
☐ d. has written

1. Al didn't study hard last year. _____, his grades were poor.

☐ a. Because
☐ b. So that
☐ c. As a result
☐ d. Since

2. If I had had more time, I could _____ you.

☐ a. have visited
☐ b. visit
☐ c. had visited
☐ d. visited

3. Jill asked me where _____ next.

☐ a. will I be gone
☐ b. would I be going
☐ c. I would being
☐ d. I would be going

4. _____ look great!

☐ a. Do ever you
☐ b. Do not you
☐ c. You do ever
☐ d. Do you ever

5. That's a _____ television.

☐ a. operated-battery
☐ b. battery-operate
☐ c. battery-operated
☐ d. battery operated

6. Will you _____ a trip this summer?

☐ a. be taken
☐ b. be taking
☐ c. taking
☐ d. are taking

7. I wish I _____ more attention in yesterday's class.

☐ a. would pay
☐ b. had paid
☐ c. could pay
☐ d. paid

8. The students did the work _____.

☐ a. themselves
☐ b. ourselves
☐ c. himself
☐ d. yourselves

9. I _____ my keys at home.

☐ a. not left
☐ b. might have left
☐ c. might left
☐ d. must left

10. Frozen dinners are convenient. _____, they don't usually taste good.
- [ ] a. Furthermore
- [ ] b. For example
- [ ] c. Thus
- [ ] d. However

11. Min and Vincent bought _____ a new car.
- [ ] a. yourself
- [ ] b. ourselves
- [ ] c. themselves
- [ ] d. yourselves

12. I'll set the alarm _____ I get up on time.
- [ ] a. so that
- [ ] b. because
- [ ] c. since
- [ ] d. thus

13. There are many ways to get downtown. _____, you can take the bus.
- [ ] a. In a word
- [ ] b. However
- [ ] c. For instance
- [ ] d. Also

14. Connie is a _____ employee.
- [ ] a. hard-work
- [ ] b. working hard
- [ ] c. hard-working
- [ ] d. hard worker

15. Luis _____ next week.
- [ ] a. getting married
- [ ] b. is getting married
- [ ] c. going to get married
- [ ] d. will married

16. I recommend that he _____ for the job.
- [ ] a. apply
- [ ] b. applies
- [ ] c. must apply
- [ ] d. applied

17. Professor Abrams _____ to speak at the conference.
- [ ] a. has invited
- [ ] b. was inviting
- [ ] c. invited
- [ ] d. was invited

18. It's essential that Juan _____ a doctor.
- [ ] a. sees
- [ ] b. will see
- [ ] c. see
- [ ] d. might see

19. _____ he is!
- [ ] a. How strange
- [ ] b. What strange
- [ ] c. How strange man
- [ ] d. Strange

20. _____ you tired of this job?
- [ ] a. Don't
- [ ] b. Won't
- [ ] c. Aren't
- [ ] d. Wouldn't

21. I won't know your schedule _____ you tell me.
- [ ] a. unless
- [ ] b. if
- [ ] c. since
- [ ] d. whether or not

22. You saw *Dick Tracy* yesterday, _____?
- [ ] a. haven't you
- [ ] b. don't you
- [ ] c. weren't you
- [ ] d. didn't you

23. You _____ called me last night.
- [ ] a. could have
- [ ] b. can have
- [ ] c. could
- [ ] d. could had

24. I was hungry because I _____ working hard all day.
- [ ] a. have been
- [ ] b. am
- [ ] c. been
- [ ] d. had been

25. Don't you think Hong's a _____ person?
- [ ] a. soft heart
- [ ] b. soft-hearted
- [ ] c. heart soft
- [ ] d. soft hearted

26. Regular exercise reduces the risk of heart disease. _____ it keeps bones and muscles in shape.
- [ ] a. Moreover
- [ ] b. On the other hand
- [ ] c. Then
- [ ] d. Therefore

27. Joe's wallet _____ on the bus yesterday.
- [ ] a. is stolen
- [ ] b. gets stole
- [ ] c. stolen
- [ ] d. got stolen

28. My boss always asks me _____ I enjoy my job.
- [ ] a. do
- [ ] b. if
- [ ] c. did
- [ ] d. that

29. The phone _____ since 9:00 A.M.
- [ ] a. has been ringing
- [ ] b. was ringing
- [ ] c. is ringing
- [ ] d. rung

30. To make a good cup of tea, first boil the water. _____, add tea leaves to the boiling water.

☐ a. Thus

☐ b. Furthermore

☐ c. Next

☐ d. However

31. Mrs. Arias called to her children, "_____ please turn off the radio!"

☐ a. Anybody

☐ b. Somebody

☐ c. Everybody

☐ d. No one

32. I met with colleagues in the morning to discuss the budget. In the afternoon, I worked hard on the annual report. In the evening, I met friends for dinner. _____, it was a busy day.

☐ a. For example

☐ b. In short

☐ c. In addition

☐ d. Furthermore

# REFERENCE KEY FOR INVENTORY TEST 2

**If you missed any items on Inventory Test 2, locate the numbers of the items on the list below and study the corresponding exercises in the Summary and Exercises section.**

| TEST ITEM | EXERCISE NUMBER | TEST ITEM | EXERCISE NUMBER |
|---|---|---|---|
| 1 | 11 | 17 | 8 |
| 2 | 1 | 18 | 24 |
| 3 | 12 | 19 | 18 |
| 4 | 20 | 20 | 19 |
| 5 | 26 | 21 | 4 |
| 6 | 22 | 22 | 17 |
| 7 | 14 | 23 | 2 |
| 8 | 7 | 24 | 16 |
| 9 | 3 | 25 | 27 |
| 10 | 30 | 26 | 29 |
| 11 | 6 | 27 | 9 |
| 12 | 10 | 28 | 13 |
| 13 | 31 | 29 | 15 |
| 14 | 25 | 30 | 28 |
| 15 | 21 | 31 | 5 |
| 16 | 23 | 32 | 32 |